Ex Libris

VICTORIAN VINEYARD

CHATEAU LOUDENNE AND THE GILBEYS

GRAND VIN
CHATEAU LOUDENNE
Grand Vin
MÉDOC
"PURITY & ELEGANCE

VICTORIAN VINEYARD

CHATEAU LOUDENNE AND THE GILBEYS

NICHOLAS FAITH

Constable

In association with Christie's Wine Publications

ISBN 0 09 465120 5

In memory of Martin Bamford
who loved and cherished Loudenne

First published in Great Britain 1983
Constable & Company Limited
10 Orange Street, London WC2H 7EG

Produced by Rock Lambert, 123 Promenade, Cheltenham, Gloucestershire

Reproduction by Cotswold Printing Company, Rodborough, Stroud, Gloucestershire
Text set in Bembo by Action Typesetting, Gloucester
Printing by Tabro Litho, St Ives, Huntingdonshire

CONTENTS

THE BEST OF BOTH WORLDS

The contributors, all of them French, to a recent book on the Médoc were asked which château of the many in the area was their favourite. 'Château Loudenne', they answered unhesitatingly, almost to a man. Given the competition from more celebrated houses, the choice might seem curious. For Loudenne is a modest country house on a medium-sized estate tucked away inconspicuously in an unfashionable northern outpost of the Médoc, 40 miles from Bordeaux.

Its charm is its position, its unpretentiousness, and its ownership. It has been in unbroken British ownership since 1875 and is thus a symbol of Britain's historic involvement in the wines of Bordeaux. At Loudenne this involvement is expressed architecturally by the solidly magnificent buildings — the 'chais' between the château and the River Gironde. They, and indeed the estate as a whole, are a tribute to the energy, flair and confidence of a Victorian family, the Gilbeys, who bought the estate over 100 years ago. That able, aggressive and feuding family kept the business, including the ownership of Loudenne, intact for 90 years.

The atmosphere of Loudenne casts a spell over the most fleeting or cynical of visitors. For the Gilbeys created a distillation of the best of both countries' traditions, combining French elegance with English informality and cosiness — a quality which pervades even the grandest of English country houses. In agricultural practice, in social life, in landscaping and in interior decoration, successive generations have built on this traditional pattern, which was ever a blend, never a compromise. The contribution made by both civilisations remains distinct and identifiable. Each provides the perfect foil for the other — like the different qualities of the merlot and cabernet sauvignon grapes in Loudenne's own wines.

The blend had already been firmly established in the 1890s, when those two stalwart Anglo-Irish literary ladies who wrote under the names of E Œ Somerville and Martin Ross stayed at Loudenne. 'The few days we spent there', they wrote, 'were like no other part of our lives . . . English management and comforts were not made incongruous by the aromatic flavour of French surroundings and the vivid pageant of the vintage; each accented the other.'*

Neither architecture nor wine provide an explanation of Loudenne's charm and uniqueness. The château itself is charming, to be sure, its unpretentious, pink-washed walls contrasting with two unimposing, almost cheeky, grey-slated turrets. Like so many other houses in the Médoc that curious, uninspiring peninsula north of Bordeaux, which produces so much great red wine from such scrubby and unpromising slopes — Loudenne is little more than a single-storied 'chartreuse', built originally in the 18th century. But where Loudenne is fortunate is that its owners, unlike those of many other Médocain estates, did not make enough money in the mid-19th century to indulge in the crenellated superstructures which ruined so many other châteaux at the time. The estate, historically, has been no more important than the house. It was never included in any of the lists of 'great growths' compiled by the Bordeaux trade, which culminated in the famous classification of 1855. Were the classification to be revised

*_In the Vine Country_, London 1893

A carved stone shield on one of the two towers at the top of each hill, north and south of the château, 'ornamented with the wyvern and castle which were the hall-mark of this remarkable family'.
Opposite: 'The drive leading up to the château is long, and in summer, usually rather dusty.'

today, Loudenne's firm yet elegant wines would certainly rank among the dozen or so 'crus bourgeois' to be elevated to the aristocracy. Even so, it is not a 'great' estate, any more than it is a 'great' house.

But it is a marvellous site, and it enjoys a unique relationship with the river that bounds the Médoc. Although the Gironde plays a dominating role in creating the geographical (and indeed geological) conditions required by the Médocain wines, the river is almost invariably invisible from its vineyards and châteaux. Loudenne is the great exception: it stands on the last major gravel-bank of the Haut-Médoc and its slopes lead down to the river itself. Where Loudenne's 'croupes' — the gravelly slopes on which its vines are grown — extend right down to the water's edge, everywhere else in the Médoc the croupes and the river are separated by a broad and often rather marshy plain — the 'palus'. Loudenne is thus possessed of a dramatic site unique in the region.

By road you come across it as you drive north from Pauillac, through a series of small and uninspiring villages: Pez, Corbian, St Seurin de Cadourne. Then, just as the rounded slopes of the Haut-Médoc slowly dwindle into a flat agricultural plain — the Bas-Médoc — there is a small lodge on the right of the twisting country road. The drive leading up to the château is long and in summer usually rather dusty; soon a wood dotted with cottages overlooks the pasture and the vines. Today the vines are largely confined to the slopes to the left between the drive and the road north to St Yzans and Lesparre; on these bumps stand toy forts, the visible symbol of the pattern imposed by the Gilbeys after they bought the estate. At the top of the hill

you are confronted by their most enduring memorial — a red brick archway, ornamented with the wyvern and castle which were the hall-mark of this remarkable family. The arch leads into a gravelled courtyard with buildings on either side: offices, garages, kitchen and hall for the harvesters. They too, are pink and low and intimate, the same age and style of architecture as the château itself.

To the Englishman the word 'château' implies grandeur — a quality entirely alien to Loudenne. From the courtyard you simply enter a small, red-tiled hallway, and through a cool and elegant drawing room catch a glimpse of the river. Then you readily understand for the first time the very particular combination which the château offers the visitor. Between the house and the swirling brown waters, successive generations have contrived to produce the ideal transitional landscape. From the château you step out onto a broad stone terrace, with 'thirty one times up and down this terrace equals one English mile' inscribed on one of the stones. This in turn is bounded by a trim hedge, which provides a token barrier against the brisk river breezes. Then comes a splendid lawn framed by magnificent trees — cypresses, chestnuts and yews — a vegetable garden renowned for generations for its strawberries and asparagus; then (a reminder that, despite the weather, despite the lawn, this is the Médoc and not Sussex) a couple of dozen rows of vines lead down into a dip, with another dozen rows up the reverse slope of the river bank.

The water is as seductive as the land. Opposite Loudenne, the Gironde, more estuary than river, is five miles of infinitely variable water, grey, brown, sometimes turbulent, rarely still, separating the Médoc shore from the low hills opposite. The slopes are gentle enough, and the river sufficiently broad, for the sky to play a full part in the view. Like the waters which reflect its moods, the clouds are endlessly changeable; the weather, as in Britain, is fickle, never routinely dull. It may be a little warmer, a trifle less rainy than the south coast of England, but the same pattern prevails. And although the Gironde is less of a watery highway today than in its 19th-century heyday, a stream of ships of all shapes and sizes passes down the deep water channel close to Loudenne.

From the river itself, the view, romantically portrayed on many a Gilbey advertisement, is dominated not by the little toy château on its equally miniature hill, but by the great black notice on the river wall: Château Loudenne, it still proudly proclaims. Behind it stretches the imposing mass of the cellars-cum-warehouses — the chais — built within a year of the purchase of the estate in 1875. Although the Gilbeys fell for Loudenne at first sight and the acquisition was in some senses a love match, at the time it made sound commercial sense. The Gilbeys purchased massive quantities of cheap claret; and in the middle of the 19th century, the Bas-Médoc was as important a source of supply as the grander slopes of the Haut-Médoc to the south of the estate. Loudenne was ideally placed as an entrepôt for their purchases. Below the warehouses, screened from the château by a row of plane trees bordering a neat gravel drive, is a little port, now rather melancholy, its cracked concrete slabs intensifying a general air of muddy neglect. But it, and its larger brother round the corner half a mile away at La Maréchale, were large enough at the time for the Gilbey's requirements.

'To the Englishman the word "château" implies grandeur — a quality entirely alien to Loudenne.'

Navigationally, these ports may have been modest. In the amount of wine passing through them, they were gigantic. In 1875, less than 20 years after they set up in business, the Gilbeys were responsible for every 20th bottle of wine consumed in Britain — six times as much as their nearest rivals. They completely dominated the scene, and deserved to: they had virtually invented a new market. The growing numbers of increasingly affluent British middle-class customers, who would never have dreamed of entering the disreputable public houses of the time, were happy enough to buy their port and their sherry, their brandy and their claret, from one of the 2,000 agents who proudly advertised their connection with the Gilbeys, the familiar red wyvern prominently displayed in their windows. Even the most upright Victorian felt a certain psychological and social reassurance in buying his drink from the local grocer.

The Gilbeys were both social and commercial revolutionaries. They alone had the wit to seize on the fiscal and legal changes introduced by the Liberal Government of 1860-61 to make wine of guaranteed quality available at a reasonable price in every town throughout the country. In due course they coined their own epithet, 'wine merchants to the people', to emphasise their intention and the scope of their ambition. They were the Victorian equivalent of Sainsburys or Marks and Spencer, names symbolising good value and guaranteed quality (and both, by no coincidence, now major forces in selling wine to a public still needing to be reassured about what it is buying).

The Gilbeys not only conferred respectability on domestic drinking. They transformed the drinking of wines of all kinds — port and sherry as much as claret and burgundy from an aristocratic affectation, confined to a few thousand customers of a handful of exclusive and expensive wine merchants into normal practice in hundreds of thousands of middle-class households. And because their fortune was founded on changes introduced by a Liberal

government, they were firmly Liberal, an astonishing (and by no means insignificant) minority in a party increasingly associated with the Temperance Movement, and certainly an anomaly within the traditionally Tory drinks business.

The purchase of Loudenne set the seal on a story of success which has few, if any, parallels, even in the vigorous and adventurous atmosphere of Victorian commerce. Although one member of the family, Walter Gilbey, acquired a baronetcy, and another, James Blyth, a peerage, their role, for all its importance — social, commercial, and personal — remains virtually unrecorded. None of the personalities involved, formidable though many of them were, rate an entry in the normally comprehensive Dictionary of National Biography. Their rise is dismissed in one line by the latest historian of drink in Victorian England. The best account of their first years is still contained in a slim celebratory volume issued in 1907, and the mass of papers they left behind has never been explored. One item only — the Diary and Visitors Book kept at Loudenne — has been transcribed and read by many subsequent visitors and writers on Bordeaux. It was the dream of the late Martin Bamford, who looked after the estate so lovingly from 1967 until his tragically early death 15 years later, to have these diaries published.

The present work has not been simply a matter of transcription or editing. This is partly because it seemed ridiculous to ignore the mass of relevant material scattered around, in England, as well as at Loudenne itself. More importantly, if anyone is to understand Loudenne, its social chemistry, its irresistible charm, not to mention its place in commercial and intellectual history, the story has to begin with the Gilbeys, their achievements, and their acumen. Without them Loudenne would have remained what it had been for hundreds of years — a backwater in the history of French wine.

WINE MERCHANTS

Henry Gilbey of Bishop's Stortford in Hertfordshire, where he owned a stage-coach running between London and his home town. Customers included the future George IV, who presented him with one of his own horses. The business was ruined by the railway and in 1842 he died leaving virtually nothing to his widow and nine surviving children.

On 14 February, 1857 a certain W L Reynolds of Bexhill answered an advertisement in the current issue of *The Liverpool Weekly Mercury.* He sent in £2 10s by Post Office Order for three bottles each of port, sherry, madeira and marsala (which together cost him £1) and a dozen bottles of brandy, which set him back £1 10s. The handwritten receipt of the money is the first entry in the first ledger kept by the two young brothers who had placed the advertisement, Walter and Alfred Gilbey. To the otherwise unknown Mr Reynolds, therefore, belongs the honour of being the first of millions of customers of the Gilbey business.

The family's connection with wine had originally been pretty tenuous: it started with Christopher Smith, a self-made wine merchant, who became Lord Mayor of London, an MP and Master of the then-mighty Drapers' Company. His wife's sister had married William Bailey, a gardener — a family legend has it that he was the Smith's own gardener and that his wife climbed out of her bedroom window to elope with him. Their younger daughter, Elizabeth, married Henry Gilbey of Bishop's Stortford in Hertfordshire. In his time Gilbey was a well-known figure, for he owned the stage-coach which ran the 30 miles between London and his home town. It was a busy route and Gilbey's customers included the Prince Regent, the future George IV, who once presented him with one of his own horses. But the business was ruined within a few months in the late 1830s by the spread of the railways, and when Henry Gilbey died in 1842, he left virtually nothing to his widow and nine surviving children.

Fortunately, the family spirit came to the rescue.

TO THE PEOPLE

Christopher Smith had already nominated Henry Gilbey's eldest son, Henry Parry Gilbey, for Christ's Hospital School, and after his father's death the young Henry Parry went to work with his mother's brother, James Bailey, in the latter's wine business. He worked there for nine years until he formed his own partnership, Southard, Gilbey, in 1851. The second son, Walter, helped James Blyth, who had married his eldest sister Catherine, to run his wine shop. At the age of 14, he was apprenticed to an uncle, who was a land agent in Tring — placed there with the help of a £50 grant from the Draper's Company, of which his great-uncle was master. He then went to work at Westminster, 'as a Parliamentary Agent', according to one account, 'as a clerk in the House of Lords', according to another. His younger brother Alfred was also taken care of within the clan and as a youngster started work with his brother and uncle in James Bailey's business. By the early 1850s, then, the family connection with the wine business was well established and in 1855 James Blyth's 14-year-old son, also called James, was apprenticed to a wine merchant who specialised in the wines from the then-British colony of the Cape of Good Hope.

The previous year Walter and Alfred had volunteered for service in the Crimean War, not as soldiers but as civilian clerks in the Army Pay Department — situations probably acquired through help from Walter's Whitehall connections. Another cousin, Henry Grinling (their mothers were sisters) was also a clerk, working for Florence Nightingale's great enemy, Dr E A Parkes. Even before their return they were probably thinking of starting in business themselves, Alfred making a detour to visit Jerez

Alfred Gilbey — negligent of dress, keen businessman, and in charge of the cellars and employees — was more importantly the tactician of the business and journalist of the partnership. A prodigious worker, he was also an unassuming philanthropist.

Walter Gilbey, the best-known and longest-lived of the partners, never single-mindedly devoted to the wine trade.

Henry Parry Gilbey — 'The Guvn'r' — Henry's eldest son, was the partners' intellectual and philosophical mentor.

and Oporto on his way back from the Crimea.

As soon as they had returned to England, the two brothers duly set up on their own, despite their total lack of financial backing. Their elder brother did not join them for six years; but for 35 years, until his death in 1893, he was to provide the partnership with its intellectual and philosophical framework. Later on Walter minimised his elder brother's role. When Henry Parry died in 1893, Walter naturally noted the fact in the Loudenne diaries, but in them Henry Parry is called simply the 'senior member of the family', not 'senior partner', and his connection with the business is dated firmly from 1863, 'six years after the business was established (in 1857) by my late brother Alfred and myself'. This is a considerable understatement of Henry Parry's role: from the beginning he visited his brothers' offices daily on his journey to work; he was invariably referred to by his younger brothers as 'The Guvn'r' — in psychological terms a substitute for the father who had died when they were children. Financially, too, his help was invaluable; from the outset the business enjoyed the crucial benefit of first-class credit facilities with the Bank of England (the partners had a special Bill Book to keep track of the many Trade Bills then used in place of cheques for foreign payments).

Henry Parry Gilbey had spotted a major gap in the market for his brothers to exploit — the growing production of cheap, reliable wines in the Cape of Good Hope.

The brothers started as they meant to continue. They sold their wines — at first through mail order — providing a guarantee of uniform quality and reasonable prices. They broke with the reticence of the older, traditional wine merchants, for from the beginning they were lavish and unashamed promoters of their products and the importance of their business. To ensure the quality they required, they imported their wines directly.

Henry Parry was himself an importer and wholesaler and could judge the tremendous advantage his brothers gained by eliminating any middlemen. The time was ripe for their initiative: the development of the steamship meant that wines could be imported more quickly and cheaply than ever before; Britain's dense railway network enabled them to deliver even single bottles swiftly and at reasonable cost throughout the country; and the growing number and affluence of the 'commercial classes' provided them with a clientèle ignored by their rivals. It took them only seven years to assemble all the elements which together constituted the 'Gilbey Revolution': the bulk import of wines direct from the country of origin; equally direct sale to the public through a network of agents; and the development of a brand name which provided a guarantee of quality, purity and value.

Like Thomas Cook, who introduced the joys of foreign travel, hitherto confined to a handful of aristocrats, to the mass of the British middle class, so the Gilbeys spread an equally important (and hitherto equally élitist) pleasure, the purchase of wines of all descriptions, among the same segment of the market.

The Gilbeys could not have made a better start. In the last three years of the 1850s, imports of wine into Britain from the Cape more than doubled, and by 1858, their first full year in business, the Gilbeys were already bringing in more than any other importer — over 55,000 gallons, enough for over half a million bottles. By the first half of 1860 — according to the figures the Gilbeys proudly published with their price lists — they were the third largest importers of wine from all sources, bringing in enough wine to fill over a million bottles.

The Gilbeys prided themselves on their direct outlets: 'extending to 25,000 Families, and upwards of 80 of the chief Hospitals, Military Messes and Public Institutions', as they boasted in 1861. But they also worked through the retail trade. In 1858, they told merchants that 'one of our representatives will wait upon you on the subject of wines from the Cape of Good Hope or South African wines . . . the time has fully arrived when these wines should be as much appreciated by the middle and commercial classes as they are by the higher and more wealthy'. The Gilbeys promised merchants profits of 20 to 25 per cent; they scorned the idea of 'the trade generally who predict that this business will not last' and who were therefore 'unwisely standing aloof from introducing these wines . . . the same prediction was doubtless freely expressed at the introduction of sherries from Spain in the earlier part of the century'.

The confident, swaggering tone was already fully developed. Within nine months of the foundation of their business, the brothers had a letter in *The Times* emphasising that the Cape was perfectly capable of producing fine wines at reasonable cost; and in the next year, in the first of the medical recommendations on which they later placed so much store, *The Lancet* chimed in with an indignant refutation of the idea that these wines 'are themselves adulterated and that they are used for adulteration'. The paper found the samples thoughtfully submitted by the Gilbeys to be 'both genuine and wholesome, while their moderate price is a great recommendation'. The emphasis on purity was crucial, for in mid-Victorian times, wines were often adulterated in some way.

The advertising, the openness, the publicity genius, all derived from Walter Gilbey. Because he survived so much longer than his brothers, because of his later fame as an authority on all manner of horses — as the saviour of the shire-horse and the founder of the Whit Monday carthorse parade in Regent's Park — he is by far the best-known of the firm's founders. But he was never single-mindedly devoted to the business: 'Circumstances made him a wine merchant, but by predilection he was a typical old English country squire', said one obituarist, 'Proud of his business, Sir Walter Gilbey had a far deeper affection for his horses', wrote another.

From his youth until his death in 1914, Walter Gilbey preserved the same stylish appearance. In person, as well as in business life, he was a great showman. The obituarists echo the description provided by the family's accountant and confidential man of business, A G Carver, who worked for them for 60 years and who, in his 80s, wrote his delightfully frank and vivid memoirs of his life with the firm. 'Walter Gilbey, tall and thin, was entirely different from his brothers, with his monocle, his special style of dress, fawn coloured waistcoat, frilled shirt and nether garments of similar cut to riding breeches'. His brother Alfred on the other hand, was 'rather negligent of his dress, generally a black morning coat and waistcoat, and dark trousers and a black bow for a tie. He was a keen business man' — nominally in charge of the cellars and the employees, but also the tactician in the business, a prodigious worker despite the bronchial trouble which carried him off in 1879, when he was only 46. It was also because of the lengthy and delightful accounts he sent home during his travels that we know so much about the early days of the Gilbey business, and his orderliness has helped historians by ensuring that they have the benefit of a mass of the business's documents.

In addition, he was a genuinely good man, much mourned as a philanthropist in the little village of Woodburn in Buckinghamshire, where he lived for 18 years (in line with his unassuming character, his obituarist noted 'an entire absence of that spirit of patronage which mars so many good actions'). But to Carver, as to everyone else, Henry Parry Gilbey, whose 'well trimmed beard and waxed moustache gave him a distinctive appearance', was 'the guiding spirit. . . . in many ways a steadying influence on the eager spirits organising the undertaking'.

The 'eager spirits' included not only the two brothers but a key group of kinsmen who became partners within a very few years. Indeed, until the late 1950s, only direct descendants of the founders ever became directors.*

---

*The only exception can be seen in a group portrait of the partners in 1867, now hanging at Loudenne. This was one Mr Langmead, a founding partner who committed suicide; not surprisingly his name is not mentioned in any of the many documents preserved by the firm or its partners, and the family name crops up only twice, so far as I can discover. A Miss Langmead lived with Alfred's family, apparently as a sort of companion or governess, and one C H Langmead visited Loudenne in 1885. Apart from that the name is forgotten.

In a single generation, a small group of families bred a team of men of varied capabilities fully equipped to run a complex and swiftly expanding business. The most important recruit was young James Blyth, 'Jim' to the family. It is a saying in the wine business that the intelligent members of the family do the buying, and within the House of Gilbey, this crucial function was entrusted largely to Alfred and to Jim, who, in Carver's words, was 'acknowledged by the trade to be very keen and an excellent judge of wines', and no mean buyer: 'Many of the visitors to the Pantheon expressed the opinion that he was a tough one to deal with'. Jim ended up with a peerage, but his prestige was earned in his constant travels of the 1860s and 1870s — accompanied by one of the Gilbeys, usually Alfred — when he forged and hardened the direct links with their suppliers all over Europe which were one of the major keys to the Gilbey's success. Unlike his cousins, Jim was not a fluent speaker: 'Though he wrote lucidly', said an obituarist, 'he had no gift of oral expression'. He was slow and even stammering of speech, and his sentences were jerky.'

A younger brother still, Henry Arthur, entered the business during its first year when still only 14, but soon took charge of the financial side of the operation. 'Short, rotund, but very active', as Carver described him, 'he was the organiser of the office and it was well done. Although he was strict with his staff he was a kind-hearted man'. Because Henry Arthur was the most private of the original partnership, the only one not active in public life, his importance was concealed. Yet one of the most crucial elements in the family's success, the rigorous quarterly stock-taking, depended on him and his brother. 'It was a

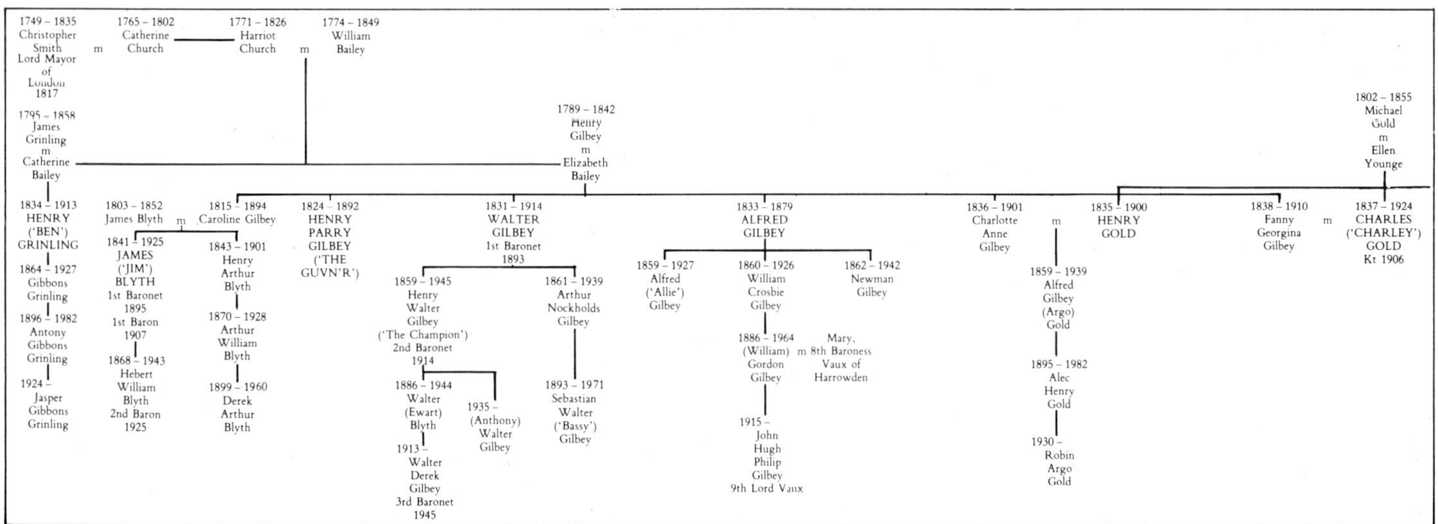

rule', wrote Carver, 'that the Books for the quarter should be balanced and the results obtained on the last day of the Quarter, which meant working till midnight. Henry Blyth was a keen worker and used to superintend the entries necessary to close the books and James Blyth personally went through all the purchases made and duty payment for the Quarter'. (Carver, who kept the Bonded Stock Book, had to stay up with them; at the time he lived at Shepherd's Bush and had to walk home at 3 am.) This financial discipline was instituted after the bad shock the partners had received at the end of 1859, when they found they had made virtually no profits, although their business had expanded greatly. It was only after a couple of stock-takings that they realised the simple truth: they had been expanding too fast for their financial soundness. From then on they never increased business at more than 20 per cent a year — although until the mid-1870s at least they never expanded at less than 10 per cent annually.

The Gilbeys were also joined by two other young men, the brothers Henry and Charles (later Sir Charles) Gold, who married the Gilbeys' two younger sisters within a couple of years of the firm's foundation. They had worked in their uncle's law stationers' business, printing Parliamentary Reports. Henry Gold (who became known as 'the solicitor' because of his fine penmanship) had come into contact with the family when he lodged with another sister, Julia, who was married to a Mr Ellis. Henry Gold had 'a genial personality. . . always cool and collected, he acted as an excellent foil to the more excitable and energetic partners'. He started on the sales side, as did his brother 'Charley', 'tall and commanding in appearance, bearded like the pard, and with fine profile', who was responsible for the Scottish business, set up in Edinburgh in 1859 — a year after his brother Henry had opened an equally successful branch in Sackville Street, Dublin. To the staff Charley 'was rather autocratic. . . . but when you got to know him no one could be more considerate', wrote Carver. To the family he was famous above all for the attention he paid to his creature comforts. Alfred wrote to his partners in Florence: 'All this beauty may be very well but we had something else to consider first, in which we would have been supported by Charley Gold had he been with us, namely the selecting of a good hotel'; a long description of the sights in the Holy City ends 'here I must leave Rome and, like Charley, see after my dinner'; and from Paris, of all places, Alfred wrote that he was following 'Charley Gold's precaution of ordering the next meal' in advance.

In the mid-1860s the clan was completed when Henry Parry finally joined the firm full-time, and their cousin Henry Grinling (known as 'Ben') resigned from the War Office to take charge of the firm's by-then-gigantic stores. Ben was 'rather of the Civil Service type', thought Carver, 'great on statistics and would come to the board meetings armed with full details of dozens of bottles and cases sent out during the week'.

For a century the tribe remained intact: 'The clan spirit is still very strong', wrote the late Alec Gold, when he completed a genealogy in the early 1950s. This shows an amazing degree of intermarriage among the Gilbeys, the Blyths and the Golds — save for the Grinlings, who married outside the family. James Blyth's daughter Gladys married Gerald Gilbey Gold; his brother Archibald married Gladys's cousin; two of Alfred's daughters repeated the pattern set by their Gilbey aunts and married two of Charley Gold's sons. More recently, the present Lord Vaux (John Gilbey) married his cousin. And even when the children married out of the clan they often formed alliances with other families in the wine business — with the Gonzalez or the Gordons of Jerez, the Hines of Cognac, or the Barrows of Corney and Barrow.

The Christian names given to the clan's numerous offspring* reflected the same inward-looking mood. There have been dozens of Walters through the generations, and one of Alfred's sons was called Newman after his godfather, the son of Christopher Smith, the founding father of the whole dynasty. They were conscious of the importance of heredity. Alfred wrote severely of one young sprig, 'I am afraid he is a Gilbey without any of the Bailey blood and will never rob a poor man of a day's work', although he softened the asperity by adding: 'He is a nice boy and I hope the bump of perseverance will develop in him as he becomes older'.

If the firm's success began on its first day in business, its transformation from a specialised firm, supplying mainly Cape wines, into an all-embracing wine business purveying every type to millions of customers, was concentrated into the first few years of the 1860s. The upheaval was triggered by a series of legislative steps by the then Liberal Government, changes which could, in theory, have helped any enterprising wine merchant. In the event, in a world grown sleepy and traditional, only the Gilbeys exploited to the full the opportunities opened by the legislators. The first step came in 1860, when the Government concluded a Free Trade Treaty with France. One result was a sharp reduction on the duty on French wines, which made them accessible to the mass of the British drinking public for the first time for 150 years. In his budget that year Gladstone, as Chancellor, sharply differentiated the duty on table wines — which were to pay only 1s a gallon — from that on port, sherry, and other fortified wines — at 2s 6d a gallon. The following year, in another effort to promote free trade in the home market, the Government enabled ordinary retailers to take out what became known as a 'grocer's licence' and sell single bottles of alcoholic liquor — an act which was immediately called 'The Single Bottle Act'.

Towards the end of his life, Gladstone wrote to the partners that he had 'always regarded the proceedings of your firm with a peculiar interest. You have been, as far as I am able to form an opinion, in an eminent sense, and in a degree with which no one can compete, the openers of the wine trade. The process has I trust, been satisfactory to yourselves; it has certainly been one highly beneficial to the country: and (like the really great enterprise of Messrs Cook) you stand outside and above the rank of ordinary commercial houses.'

Gladstone was a shrewd observer and also a canny politician: in the same letter — which was to thank the Gilbeys for having found some 'astringent wine' recommended by his doctors and not otherwise available — he makes the point that 'I should myself long ago have

*Between them Walter and Alfred Gilbey and the Gold brothers produced 41 offspring who lived long enough to marry and produce children of their own.

carried to you my insignificant custom, but for my systematic disinclination to part company with those whom I have long known and dealt with'. He knew of the rumours that he had profited from the changes but could do nothing to stop them, except to take the elementary precaution of not buying his wines from the Gilbeys. This did not help. A generation later, the Old Man's son, Viscount Gladstone, wrote that 'the story was spread about, and widely believed, that Mr. Gladstone was a partner in Gilbey's or at least had some interested connection with that famous firm. After I entered Parliament, I had myself frequently to contradict these false allegations. I have reason to think that the "Gilbey" invention still persists'.*

The Gilbeys claimed, reasonably enough, that any other firm could have taken equal advantage of the changes: in their Circular dated April 1862 — just after Gladstone had announced his latest budgetary changes — the partners boasted of a sales increase against the previous year of 30 per cent in 1861** and remarked that the pace was being maintained, claiming a 'total delivery from our stores of more than 1,300 dozen of wines and sprits weekly. Only five years since, that was considered an extraordinary business which included as much as 100 dozen a week, but numerous instances of proportionate success have come to our knowledge in the case of houses which have adopted liberal principles similar to those it has been our study to infuse into the conduct of our several establishments.'

The Gilbeys remained loyal to the party for a generation. Charley Gold became a Liberal MP; Walter Gilbey was granted his baronetcy and Jim Blyth his peerage by Liberal governments grateful for their support, financial as well as political; and, although Alfred was made a Justice of the Peace by Disraeli, he was as staunch a supporter of Gladstone and the Liberal cause as the rest of the clan.

The Gilbeys immediately seized on the opportunities Gladstone offered them to reduce the price of French wines. In the late 1850s they had been selling vin ordinaire from Bordeaux at 30s a dozen, yet by 1st January 1861 they were advertising that, because of a final reduction of wine duties, sound dinner clarets were available at 14s, a price they reduced to 12s a case, 1s a bottle within a couple of years. They were not alone — wine imports in 1860 jumped by 50 per cent to nearly 12½ million gallons — but they were quick off the mark, and followed through their success in two crucial ways: they introduced a uniform brand name for everything they sold, and, after some delay, enlisted the help of over 2000 of Britain's most respectable tradesmen to sell their products.

Until 1863 or so the Gilbeys had labelled their brands solely with numbers branded on the cork. The most expensive claret was described simply as 'Southard's own Growth — of his celebrated vintage'. This wine, they went on, 'irrespective of name or district, is certainly as fine as can be desired; it has great body, full colour with a delicate bouquet' (by 1861 the Gilbeys were outselling their supplier six to one). It was only in 1863 that they adopted

The Victorian grocers formed the bulk of the 2000 links in the Gilbey's chain of agents in Britain.

**After 30 years* by Viscount Gladstone, Macmillan 1928

**In reality the figure was nearer 20 per cent.

MATTHEW & SON
The STORES.
TRINITY STREET.

GOODWIN, FOSTER, BRO
G.F.B.Lᵈ
PROVISION STORES.
AND TEA EXCHAN
GOODWIN · FOSTER · BROWN
FOSTER BROWN LIMITED
OODWIN FOSTER

QUALITY & VALUE—No better guarantee can be given than the fact that about every tenth bottle of Wine and thirty-third bottle of Spirits consumed in the United Kingdom is supplied through W & A Gilbey's Agents.

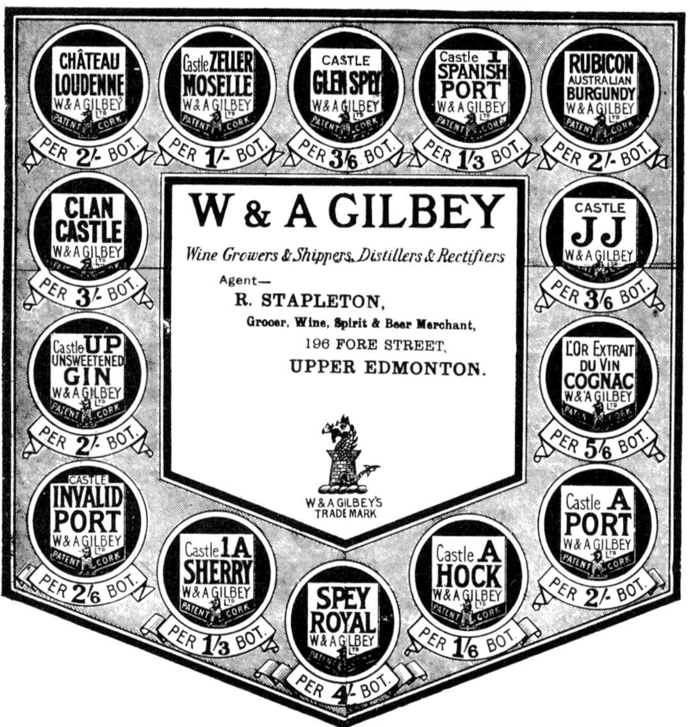

'In each town a few select grocers (or licensed chemists or tea merchants) had the right to the agency. The only alcoholic drink they could sell was Gilbey's'. The network soon grew to over 2,000 names.

their famous Castle label, 'whereon, wrote an admiring journalist in *The Illustrated London News,* 'is depicted the familiar griffin*, "swinging his tail as a gentleman switches his cane" out of the door of the diminutive castle in which he is confined'. Other merchants advertised 'The Chancellor's claret' at 1s a bottle, but it was the Gilbeys distribution system which gave it the unflattering soubriquet 'Grocer's claret', to go with 'Grocer's port'.

According to the family's official history, published in 1907, it was the grocers of a number of provincial towns who made the first overtures to the Gilbeys, and gave them the idea of taking advantage of the 'Single Bottle Act' of 1861, which had for the first time allowed ordinary retailers to sell drink in small quantities. Previously the Gilbeys had claimed the credit for the initiative. 'Although at the time of the passing of the Single Bottle Act', they wrote in one of their annual circulars to their agents, 'we had some fifty thousand private customers and our average weekly sales exceeded fifteen hundred dozens, we became convinced that sufficient attention had not hitherto been given to the importance of local convenience in obtaining wines and spirits of reliable quality. With this view, we decided to take up fresh ground and to assume rather the position of collectors of the produce of the various wine producing countries, and look to Agencies as the means of distribution throughout the United Kingdom.'

They soon systematised their agency system. In each town a few select grocers (or licensed chemists or tea merchants) had the right to the agency. The only alcoholic drink they could sell was Gilbey's. Their margins were

* In reality a wyvern

fixed. They bought at trade prices (less a small agency discount), and had to sell at prices set by the Gilbeys. The family's tight control over the network, which soon grew to over 2000 names, was evident in the vast leather-bound ledgers in their head office, in which every transaction with every one of them was scrupulously recorded. The agents had to pay within seven days of the end of the month (with an additional discount as a reward for prompt payment) and, like the members of many such networks since, suffered from having the successful amongst them held up as an example to the rest. The Gilbeys, in listing agents whose sales exceeded £250 in a quarter, even gave the size of the town in which the agent operated, to emphasise the relative degree of success. It was obviously easier for Messrs Dakin Shinton to extract £924 6s from the 147,000 inhabitants of Wolverhampton, than for Mr Salmon to sell £848 15s 5d worth to the 25,000 inhabitants of Reading (both were among the three pioneers of the system).

The Gilbeys' unique system — of exclusive agents working on fixed margins — also had the advantage of eliminating the then widespread practice of 'loss-leading' — offering some staple product at or below cost to attract customers into a store (sugar had been the first product to be used in this way). And, as the Gilbeys pointed out in one of their confidential circulars, 'the system on which our Agencies are established is a great safeguard against unfair competition. . . . as the prices of all our goods are fixed and it is not open therefore to a neighbouring trader to undersell, at perhaps little or no profit, our Wines and Spirits, as is too often done in the case of packed, tinned, and other proprietary articles'. They were, effectively, pioneers of the system of retail price maintenance, providing protection especially for their smaller agents.

In return, the Gilbeys provided an enormous degree of back-up. The agents did not have to stock more than a few of the most widely sold wines, for the partners claimed that they had two dozen cases of all their best-selling varieties ready packed for immediate despatch anywhere within the British Isles (mixed cases were normally only sent in mid-month).

If the agent did not make enough out of the agency to cover the cost of the various government licences he required (by no means negligible at over £24 a year) then the Gilbeys, confident of the success of their formula, would make up any losses. But most support was more positive. The agents were regularly guided on the intricacies of obtaining and renewing their precious licences from magistrates (who often grew restless because their powers of refusal were so limited). They were provided with a wide variety of advertising material, 'railway tablet, show board, Window papers and Bin tickets for leading Wines and Spirits', special window papers for Christmas — and an offer to pay half the cost when agents advertised between September and Christmas.

An even more crucial advantage was access to the Gilbeys' incomparable range of wines, which soon grew to include over 200 different varieties of drink. They were all called by the Castle name, accompanied by a letter — A being invariably the cheapest. There were 27 different sherries, eight ports, five varieties of marsala, three of madeira, gin (at 2s a bottle), 10 clarets, six of which were 'old in bottle', and seven sauternes at from 15s to 105s a dozen. The most expensive was 'wine produced on the Chateau Yquem estate. It is the growth of one of the best succeeded years' — a remark which takes the breath away. Here was a group of young men established in business less than a decade, using their own brand name rather than one of the most distinguished names in the whole world of wine. But they did not forget other tastes. Malaga was boosted: 'its low alchoholic strength and moderate price render it a most suitable wine for sacramental purposes'. There were eight champagnes, including 3A, 4A and 5A (the 'A's were dry, plain numbers indicating a 'fruity' fizz), four sparkling burgundies and a red hock, a dozen foreign liqueurs and the same number of British varieties, as well as wines from Hungary, and 'Tent' from Spain; and of course the Cape of Good Hope, the Gilbeys' early staple, which was soon relegated to the bottom of the list of imports.

The Gilbeys churned out their lists by the hundred thousand and instructed their agents to stamp them with their name and circulate them regularly and systematically to the more respectable inhabitants of their town. (The Bodleian Library at Oxford has a dozen such lists in it, presumably deposited there by dons who had previously satisfied their requirements.) By the 1890s (albeit before the days of universal male suffrage, and when women had no votes) everyone on the voters' lists in the United Kingdom had been circulated and 'we are now engaged in going over the ground again'.

Circulars, they urged, could also usefully be sent to the ever-increasing numbers of candidates for 'County Councils, School Boards, and various other local official positions — in addition to candidates for Parliament', all 'only too anxious to obtain their requirements from local Traders'.

The list and the endless adjurations were not the firm's only publications. They did not advertise directly, but every year they reported on the vintage in Bordeaux in a long letter to *The Times.** In 1869 they published what amounted to a scholarly text book on the 'Wines of the Principal Producing Countries'. Contemplating this mass of material, Carver wondered 'whether even in those spacious days, the tradesmen found time to read, mark and digest so many details of a subject of which so little is known by British tradesmen'.

Naturally, other merchants tried to insinuate their products into the Gilbeys' agents. This produced a splendid blast. 'Selling wines and spirits other than ours', thundered the partners, 'would not only be breaking the faith with us but it would be equivalent to stating that our goods are not equal in value to other descriptions, a proceeding which would certainly tend to destroy confidence in the agent on the part of his customers'. One subversive pretending to be one of their travellers, although probably acting for their rivals, went round urging agents to ask for better credit terms (which would have severely strained the Gilbeys' finances).

The Gilbeys needed all the support they could get against the wide variety of forces arrayed against them. They enlisted their agents against the railway companies, who

*An idea they probably got from *The Illustrated London News*, a favourite vehicle for favourable articles on their activities. There is an 1854 issue of the publication in the Gilbey archives containing an account of that year's vintage.

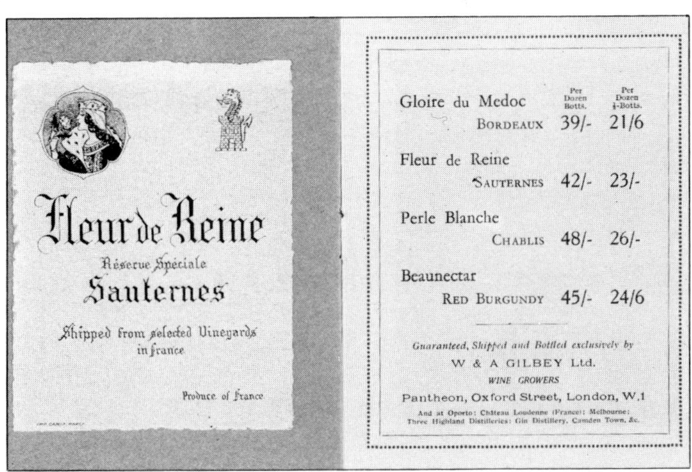

The Gilbey publicity machine — the emphasis always on 'good quality, good value' — churned out lists, circulars, medical advice and statistics.

Influenza Epidemic

DURING the Influenza epidemic of last year the Medical Profession prescribed with the most marked success the undermentioned brands of W & A Gilbey which have been specially prepared for the use of Invalids.

These Wines were found to be so efficacious a remedy for the Influenza, that the demand for them last year alone actually exceeded Two Hundred Thousand Bottles, as will be seen from the following figures.

INVALID PORT	135,408	Bottles
QUININE SHERRY	40,152	"
TONIC PORT (Malt & Meat)	18,192	"
INVALID CHAMPAGNE ...	11,352	"
	205,104	

[TURN OVER

tried to increase rates on the thousands of small shipments made by the Gilbeys. (Some railway companies even tried to set themselves up as direct buyers of wines and spirits for their refreshment rooms and hotels.) More important opponents included the ever-growing temperance lobby (usually active members of the Liberal Party to which they owed so much), aristocratic wine merchants sneering at Gilbeys' offerings, and the powerful lobby represented by the brewers and publicans — the 'licensed victuallers'. These were always referred to by the Gilbeys as 'the monopolists', so as to associate themselves with free trade, that most powerful of Victorian causes.

The 'social' attacks disguised their rivals' fury at the Gilbeys' only-too-successful attack on their profit margins. But they were usually clothed in decidedly snobbish gloves. In *The American Senator,* Trollope outlines a typical attitude:' ''In the States we haven't got into the way yet of using dinner clarets'', says the Senator of the title,''your great statesman added much to your national comfort when he took the duty off the lighter kinds of French wines'' '. The reply sums up the forces arrayed against the Gilbeys: 'The rector could not stand it. He hated light wines. He hated cheap things in general. And he hated Mr Gladstone in particular. ''Nothing'', said he, ''that the statesman you speak of ever did could make such wine as that any cheaper. I am sorry, sir, that you don't perceive the difference.'' '

The Gilbeys counter-attacked in a dozen different ways. They repeatedly emphasised the sheer convenience of their system and the undoubted fact that their products were 'of uniform good quality . . . good value at the prices charged'. They faced agents who complained, even at the end of the 1870s, that they did not 'get their fair proportion of the trade of what are termed the ''upper classes'' '. Forget them, said the Gilbeys in effect: 'this particular trade is mostly done through personal influence, and by much personal solicitation, while it is not so much to be coveted, being extremely uncertain and vacillating'. The Gilbeys emphasised that the good value they offered would ensure that their products came first.

They went much further than that, however. They enlisted the medical profession whenever their jealous rivals alleged that the Gilbeys were selling adulterated wines, since their prices could never cover pure ones. As early as January 1862 Murray Thompson, MD, FCS, a lecturer in chemistry at the Edinburgh Medical school, then possibly the most famous in the country, was sent three samples of the Gilbeys' cheaper clarets to test. He duly pronounced that 'from a medical point of view, I have every confidence in recommending such wines, as above, as wholesome articles of diet. They are genuine and pure, and as far as I am capable of judging they are really what they are represented to be. The amount of alcohol which they contain is such as to render the drinking of them in ordinary amounts quite harmless.'

Carver quotes a typically worried note in the list of a Plymouth wine merchant: 'We observe that some houses continue to quote Claret at 12s a dozen, bottles and cases included. No good wine can be sold at this price, except at a loss.The wine is acid, coloured or mixed with water, or perhaps all three.' To which the *London Medical Record* replied stoutly: 'We have taken some pains to verify the correctness of the guarantee given by W & A Gilbey and are bound to say, that we find the wine to be perfectly sound pure and wholesome French wine.' When all else failed, the Gilbeys could always fall back on Dr Druitt, author of a book on cheap wines, which contained one crucial passage: 'Bordeaux wines are of special service: they neither turn sour themselves, nor are they the cause of sourness in other articles of food. They increase the appetite, they exhilarate the spirits, and they tend to fill the veins with pure healthy blood.'

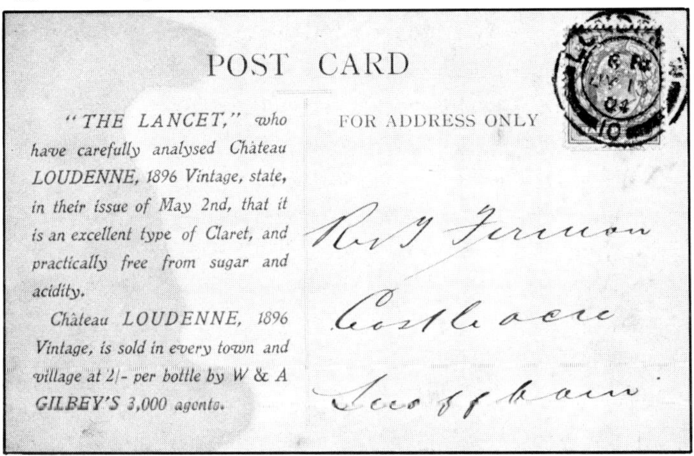

Indeed, the Gilbeys always emphasised how many of their products were of positive medical value. 'Owing to its rapid action as a stimulant and restorative', they claimed, 'champagne has obtained a high position in the opinion of the medical profession, and in cases of great prostration or exhaustion it is highly valued, as its action is more immediate and harmless than that of brandy'. They even sent out a 'Special Circular relative to wines for the use of invalids, the issue of which at the present time when the influenza is unfortunately again causing so much illness, cannot fail to do good'.

Politically they mobilised their agents in the Off Licence Holders Protection Association, which allowed their most trusted chief agent to dispense sums of money to carefully selected parliamentary candidates. In 1874, a bill was introduced to stop the issue of any further licences. 'We do not anticipate that the Government will support such a proposal', the partners wrote to their agents, 'but, considering the strength of the Publicans and the Teetotal party in the House of Commons, there is some danger to be apprehended.' The trusty 2000 were urged to communicate their views to their Member of Parliament, either personally or by letter.

Later in the decade the Gilbeys mobilised even greater forces. They organised a mammoth petition, signed by '12 noblemen and titled personages, 10 members of Parliament, 140 justices of the peace, 138 officers of the army and navy, 730 members of the clergy, 823 doctors, 1595 gentry and 6050 merchants, tradesmen and others', to testify that the growth of off-licences had been 'an important convenience to the public, and has tended to the decrease of intemperance more especially among the middle classes, by whom at present this branch of trade is chiefly supported'.

Although they introduced some rather dubious-sounding 'house-hold spirits', designed 'to meet the requirements of consumers in the large mining and manufacturing districts and poorer neighbourhoods', yet, as Henry Parry Gilbey testified to a Committee of the House of Lords, contrary to the general impression, the Gilbeys had no agencies in such areas. Gilbey deplored the fact. It meant that these neighbourhoods, as well as 'smaller towns and all the large villages are entirely shut out from what I should call consumption through a reliable medium' — since the size of licence fees meant that only substantial towns could support a Gilbey agent.

'The Guvn'r' was giving the evidence to a House of Lords Select Committee on Intemperance — one of an interminable series of inquiries into the subject, which occupied so much parliamentary time during the Victorian age. This particular inquiry provided him with a splendid platform from which to state the basic Gilbey defence against charges that they encouraged drunkenness — especially amongst women, in Victorian eyes especially at risk from the smallest drop. He faced the accusations squarely and fairly. 'I have not been able to trace a single case which has been quoted here', he said flatly, 'although I have taken down nearly every case which has been mentioned, and sent down to the country town where it was said to have occurred, I have never been able to trace it to the point'.

His basic theme was simple. It was not drink itself that was the problem. 'It is the bad distribution, the unhappy mode and places in which drink is taken, and the want of knowledge people have of the alcohols they take, coupled with the misfortune of having the traffic allied to a monopoly; we told you that France drank more alcohol per head than England, and that if double the consumption in England took place at home it could be taken with perfect safety and be enjoyed.' Consumption at home, he said persuasively, was 'calculated to produce, or at least tend to temperance, because whatever is drunk is consumed in the presence of those who are most careful about their economy and their temperance. Moreover it is drunk in participation and the drinking of it is spread over a longer period of time: and again, I think as a rule it would be drunk with meals.' His point of view won the day. The Committee's conclusion was decisive: 'No evidence has been given that the Retail of wine under the Refreshment-house and Wine Licence Acts has increased intemperance: on the contrary, it has been urged with a considerable show of reason, that the operation of these Acts, besides affording much convenience to the public, has had a beneficial effect in encouraging the use of light wines instead of stronger beverages.'

An even more conclusive judgement came the next year from their old benefactor. In his 1880 Budget Speech Mr Gladstone declared: 'Since the wine duties were altered fundamentally in 1860, great progress has been made in facilitating the consumption of wine, cheap wine, and of sound wine throughout the country. The Character of the Trade has been fundamentally changed — adulteration is greatly diminished, and the consumption of sound wine and of cheap wine has been very greatly increased.'

Not even the Gilbeys dared quote this particular encomium to their efforts.

The basic Gilbey defence against charges that they encouraged drunkeness — especially amongst women — was that while 'consumption at home was calculated to produce temperance', 'the unhappy places in which drink is taken' encouraged intemperance.

BASS
ALE

PANTHEON

AND ROUNDHOUSE

The flair which informed every aspect of the Gilbeys' activities was symbolised by the properties they acquired to accommodate their ever-expanding business. Within 15 years of the firm's establishment, sales had risen to over nine million bottles a year and considerable room was required to store, bottle and despatch 200,000 bottles every week, as well as to oversee the activities of over 2,000 agents. It was not, however, in the family's nature to content itself with anonymous offices or characterless warehouses. Both offices and stores became further weapons in the Gilbey armoury, handsome and practical advertisements for the business.

They started with a modest office at the corner of Berwick Street and Oxford Street, on the northern edge of Soho. Within a couple of years they had moved to larger premises at 357 Oxford Street (which later, appropriately enough, became a wine bar). No sooner had they moved than they were casting envious eyes on a once-famous establishment a few doors down the street. '357 Oxford Street (three doors from Pantheon)', was how they described it on their note paper, and in 1867, 10 years after they had started their business, they annexed the Pantheon itself on a 28-year lease. They bought the freehold a few years later, and were not to leave it until 1937, when they sold the building to Marks and Spencer.

The Pantheon, a handsome, porticoed building, was designed by James Wyatt and opened in 1772 as one of that long-vanished breed of pleasure domes for the enjoyment of the British aristocracy: 'A place of evening entertainment for the Nobility and Gentry', proclaimed the proprietors, who tried to keep out undesirable ladies by refusing to

Left and below: Within a couple of years they had moved to larger premises at 357 Oxford Street. Opposite page: No sooner had they moved than they were casting envious eyes on the Pantheon, three doors away. Ten years after they had started their business, they annexed the Pantheon itself.

admit female subscribers unless they were recommended by peeresses. Subscribers were provided with a monthly entertainment diet of concerts, balls and masquerades. The Pantheon was soon patronised by the Prince of Wales (later George IV) and his royal brothers, and under their influence the place went downhill — morally rather than socially. The slide quickened when the building was gutted by fire 20 years after it opened, leaving only Wyatt's shell intact. It was rebuilt, but never again regained its former position, and in the 1830s opened as bazaar and art gallery.

Its renaissance was to be at the hands of the Gilbeys, for 'this apartment, as imposing as the interior of any first-class London bank', was to become their headquarters. They transformed the Pantheon: the former gallery became 'a spacious hall . . . desks succeeding desks, of the shiniest mahogany with bright brass rails, ground-glass screens, rows of vellum-covered ledgers'. Carver remembered how at the end of this enormous circular space was the Board Room, 'a very spacious room having a semi-circular appearance caused by handsome pillars of Corinthian design, and a very lofty domed roof'. To one side was a sample room and an office for interviewing agents. In the early days, 'many of them had no bank accounts and brought notes and gold in payment. Agents from distant parts of the country would send up £5 notes cut in half, one half sent first, the second sent the next day.' One of Carver's first jobs was to 'stick the two parts together with stamp paper'.

Carver himself worked at the Pantheon for 60 years, keeping the partners' private accounts as well as acting as the firm's accountant. When he retired, he was succeeded

Opposite: 'as imposing as the interior of any first-class bank . . desks succeeding desks, of the shiniest mahogany'.

first by his son and then by his grandson, who retired only in 1981.* Such continuity was not unusual in what remained for a long time a truly 'family firm'. The partners had a special fund for long-serving employees fallen on hard times. In the 90 years after Charley Gold established the Edinburgh business, for instance, it had only three managers; and in 1945 there were nine men working in the firm who had been there 50 years before.

But the firm was by no means a benevolent society: the partners' files are full of disciplinary cases, of men dismissed for petty peculations, or that ever-present temptation, getting into the habit 'of running round the corner', in

*My many quotations from his grandfather's memoirs come from a copy kindly lent me by John Carver.

Above: 'the partners claimed that they had two dozen cases of all their best-selling varieties ready packed for immediate despatch anywhere within the British Isles'.
Opposite, top: The printing department, formerly the main hall of the Pantheon bazaar. 'A vast space, some hundred foot square . . . devoted exclusively to the work of the firm, and giving employment to about 140 hands, and where 12 cylinder machines are incessantly throwing off bills, placards, invoices, circulars, price lists, trade notes and labels of various kinds.'
Opposite, bottom: 'Physically the best known feature was the "Roundhouse", merely one of the Gilbeys' three bonded warehouses' on the Camden site.

Carver's words, 'to see a Man about a dog'. The particular unfortunate he mentioned, Tommy Gilbert, 'as artful as a wagon load of monkeys . . . was noted for his tight trousers. 'Twas said his landlady had to pull them off at night and that he used a shoehorn to get into them'.

Carver's memoirs are full of such vignettes, conjuring up a rich picture of late Victorian office life, full of minor ceremonies and major inconveniences. 'The office was illumined by gas standards to each desk while the domed roof had two large starlights which were lit from below by one of the porters named Palmer. He was a fine-looking old chap with a beard, and he would appear in his uniform of bottle green coat, at lighting up time, with a long pole at the end of which was a brass fitting, to which was attached a taper, which was lit. The big end of the pole was steadied against a desk and raised to an upright position and balanced, and the starlights were lit up. This operation was a daily source of delight to the Staff who watched every moment, in case the pole should fall. Old Palmer never made a mistake.' But if the lighting was infallible, the heating certainly wasn't. The stove in the middle of the enormous hall had been ordered by Sir Robert Peel just before he died and never delivered. 'It had two fireplaces, a down draught being created by lighting fires in the basement. At certain times, when the wind was in the east, the down draught failed and the Office would be filled with smoke. A hurried attack on the fires led to them being cleared out and one shivered in the cold.'

Below the office was the printing department, formerly the main hall of the Pantheon bazaar. 'A vast space', wrote the awestruck *Illustrated London News,* 'some hundred foot square . . . devoted exclusively to the work of the firm, and giving employment to about 140 hands, and where 12 cylinder machines are incessantly throwing off bills, placards, invoices, circulars, price lists, trade notes, and labels of various kinds'. Below, 'after a glance at the deserted aviary . . . we descend to the lower vaults. Here are stowed away some 40,000 dozen of the choicer vintages of France, Spain, Portugal, Germany and Hungary, in solidly-built cellars, extending right under the building and constructed fully a hundred years ago.'

Even this massive stock was not nearly enough to service the Gilbeys' normal requirements; by the time of the article

they were despatching nearly 200,000 bottles of wines and spirits to their customers every week. The biggest category, 'Sherries, Marsalas and other light wines', accounted for over 40,000 bottles, ports and brandies for 32,500 each. They sold over 25,000 bottles of their gin weekly, 20,000 bottles of whiskey (mostly Irish) and nearly as much claret 'and other light wines'.

To store and despatch such enormous quantities — reaching a peak of over 1,500,000 bottles every December — required a correspondingly impressive set up. Gilbey's gigantic stores and gin distillery were sited on railway land between Camden Town and Chalk Farm, a couple of miles north of the Pantheon. When Carver first arrived thay were connected only by a 'Wheatstone Transmitter', a primitive ancestor of the telephone, which was installed in 1877 (the Gilbeys must have been early customers of the then Telephone Company). The Camden stores were presided over by the bureaucratic Henry Grinling, who had as his righthand man F S Plowright, 'an efficient exponent of the Civil Service type for statistical information'.

The Camden operation made even the most cynical gasp. By any standards it was enormous, and it employed a wide variety of highly ingenious machinery. Physically its best-known feature was the 'Roundhouse',* the former engine shed of the London and North Western Railway. The Roundhouse was merely one of Gilbey's three bonded warehouses on the site.

The whole operation covered an acre and a quarter, and the five acres of flooring used in the 1870s had quadrupled by the first decade of the century. Visitors marvelled at the steam lift employed to move the casks, 'shooting them up in the manner of a jack-in-the-box'. They wondered at the bottle department, with 84 vats each containing 1,500 or more gallons of spirits, and 17 monsters with 10,000 gallons apiece. Fifty 'nimble youths . . . displaying the activity of demons in a pantomime' were required to wash all the 50,000 bottles required every day. Despite their nimbleness 10 tons of broken glass had to be cleared away from the bottle department each week.

Two floors below was another amazing sight: 'Passing down passage after passage', wrote *The Illustrated London News,* 'some almost dark, others partially lighted by reflector-backed gas-jets, the mind grows fairly bewildered at the amount of claret in casks, in bins, and in cases on all sides. Clarets in casks to the amount of 2,000 hogsheads; clarets in bins that are really huge vaulted apartments, each holding several thousand dozen; claret for transport in cases built up into solid blocks. By the aid of the gaslight we discern cellarmen engaged in drawing off wine from the casks and adding to the stacks of bottles, several of which are composed of a solid mass of from 2,000 to 5,000 dozen, with strips of oak between each layer. The bins thus built up repose in peace for at least twelve months, and are then distributed broadcast over the land.' Indeed probably the most remarkable feature of the whole operation was that a train, known inevitably as the Gilbey Special, was required to deliver one day's sales of this extraordinary firm.

Opposite: The Roundhouse on the horizon of the Gilbey bottling and bonded warehouse colossus in Camden.

*In the late 1950s, Jasper Grinling, Ben Grinling's great-grandson, arranged for its transfer to a trust which adapted the buidling for use as a theatre.

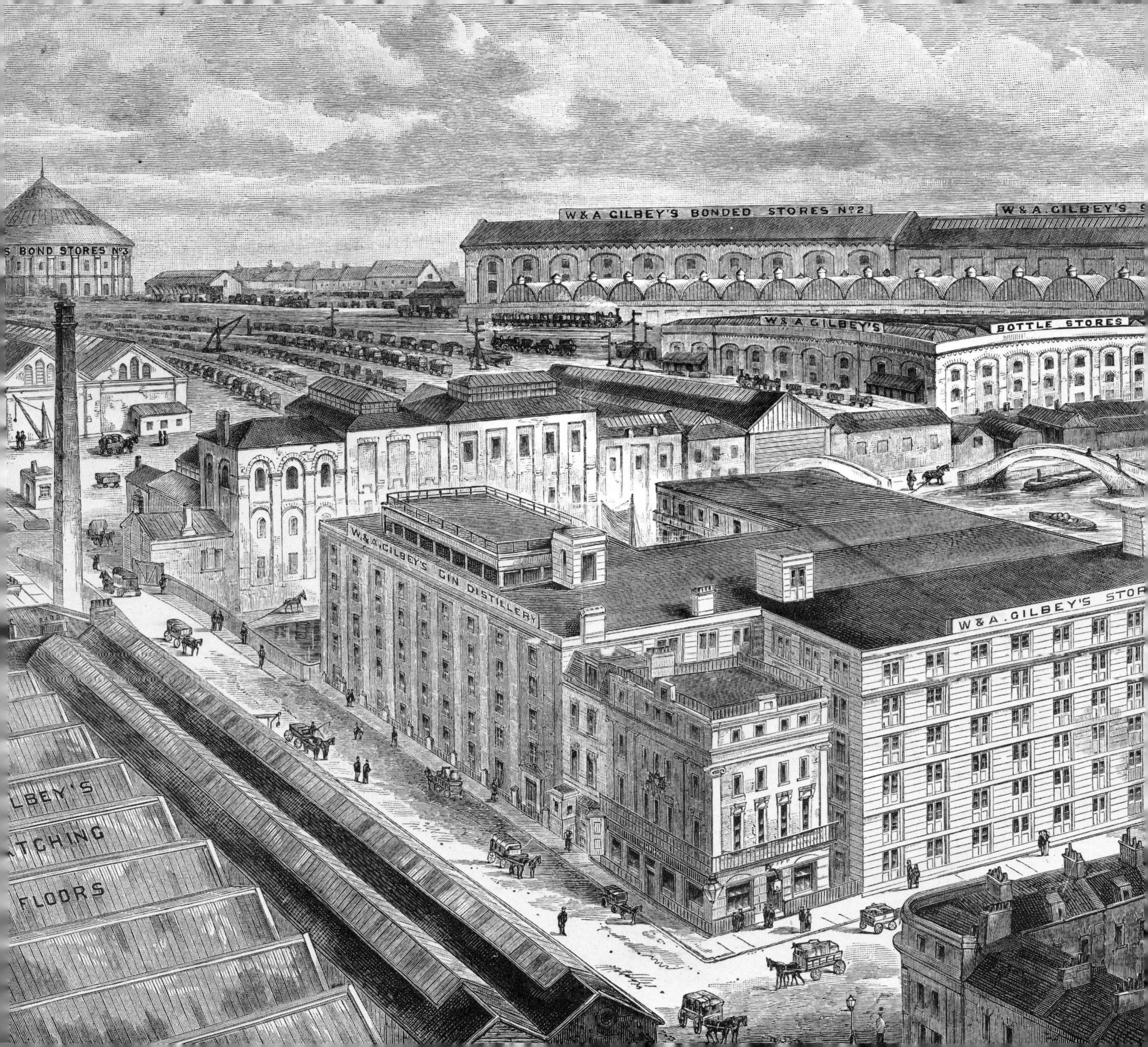

W & A GILBEY'S BONDED STORES No 2
W & A. GILBEY'S
S BOND STORES No 3
W & A GILBEY'S
BOTTLE STORES
W & A. GILBEY'S GIN DISTILLERY
W & A. GILBEY'S STOR
LBEY'S
TCHING
FLOORS

Royal Marsala
CASTLE A
5 years old
Castle A
MARSALA
W & A GILBEY
LTD
BRAND ON CORK
Bottled & Guaranteed by
W&A Gilbey
LTD

SHERRY Oro
2A
4 Years Old
Bottled and Guaranteed by
W&A Gilbey
LTD
IMPORTED FROM
JEREZ DE LA FRONTERA-SPAIN

OPORTO BLANCO
FROM PORTUGAL
Bottled and
Guaranteed by
W&A Gilbey

THE ROAD TO LOUDENNE

In order to keep their Camden Town colossus supplied, the Gilbeys bought direct from the wine-growing districts, so they naturally visited their suppliers with some regularity. From 1863 on (usually more than once a year), the partners roamed Europe in pairs to keep their suppliers up to the mark. The most frequent partnership was that of Alfred Gilbey and James Blyth. The two-month trip they undertook in the spring of 1874 — an account of which is fortunately preserved at Loudenne — was unusual. It took longer than normal, since the partners visited Marsala in Sicily for the very first time, as well as taking in Burgundy, Jerez and Oporto, returning through Bordeaux. Moreover it is clear from the copious account — the Travelling Journal — written by Alfred early every morning that it was on this trip that he finally decided that the firm needed a base in France, and it was this decision which led to the purchase of Loudenne the following year.

Alfred Gilbey clearly identified himself with the great mass of his middle-class clientèle, and was deeply suspicious of the pretensions of members of the commercial classes encountered abroad. He rather despised one shipper in Oporto, with two sons in the Army and the other 'just proceeding to Cambridge from Harrow' — and who, moreover, left the actual selling of his wines to his partners. 'The old gentleman,' he wrote, 'is very rich but a little above his business — I expect riches are very apt sometimes to have this effect.' (Ironically, when Alfred himself died, only five years later, he left £350,000 — worth comfortably over £10 million in modern money.) But Alfred did not think of himself as well-off.

Alfred (who refers to himself throughout as 'A G') was more conscious of his nationality than of his class. Late at night in bandit-infested Palermo, 'we got back to the hotel at 11.30 not having been stopped on the way although we are told that the outskirts of Palermo are anything but safe — our nationality may perhaps have something to do with it'. Being English cost more but meant you didn't have to learn any foreign language. One eager young salesman in Palermo, is described as a 'dark good looking chap, but when I found that the fool did not speak English I dropped him like a hot potato'.

Yet, in a way we might now think of as un-English, A G was open about his feelings. When he saw the Bay of Naples he lamented, 'had I a spark of poetry about me I ought here to break forth in raptures and do the sublime . . . I feel it all that if I try to put my feelings in action up comes the choking sensation of swallowing nothing'. And the first glimpse of Rome was enough to knock him off his perch: 'In our commercial England we ignoramuses are very apt to look too lightly on classical attainments — never before did I feel so ignorant as I have done since the few hours that I have been in this ancient city, Rome.'

But their minds invariably reverted to the business. In Pompeii the party duly inspected the riskier frescoes, but lingered longer over the wine merchants' shops. These 'appeared very numerous and evidently combined the oil trade and on an equally large scale — the shops were fitted with stone earthenware jars built into massive brick counters — some of the jars had actually the makers' names on them'. In his tour round Jerez a few weeks later A G spotted that 'to my astonishment here these receptacles were large earthenware ones holding from 2 to 3 butts made in the shape of the old oil jars that you see at Pompeii'.

The pace was amazing. A G occasionally complained of his age and referred casually to the pills he needed to take. He also suffered excruciating bouts of sea-sickness. The worst was on the voyage from Sicily to Malta on their — rather roundabout — way to Jerez. 'We did not reach Malta', wrote A G, 'till between 11 and 12, nearly five hours later — the Captain says he never knew such weather before in May it being weather they sometimes get in December and January.' Once they left the harbour, 'the sickness came on and lasted the whole night taking everything from me including at the last some black stuff that I cannot account for'.

But they were not deterred by such experiences. Typically on one day in Sicily, they rose at five, rode for two and a half hours over rough roads in a bumpy carriage, embarked on an eight-hour steamer trip (on which the vibrations of the ship's screw gave A G a clammy kind of feeling) only to change into dress suits at their destination and bump over a further three miles of rough road before dinner. All-night journeys in primitive trains were normal: the 27-hour trip from Cordoba to Oporto is described simply as 'capital'; and the civil war against the Carlists had so dislocated travel that a 44-hour journey to Valencia is dismissed as 'a most wonderful journey in the present state of Spain'. Nevertheless, the unprecedented length of the journey took its toll. By the time they left Jerez, A G wearily recorded that 'if we ever get back a fortnight's journey will appear to us a mere flea bite: we are getting fearfully homesick and ought to have left out Oporto on this journey'.

Despite all the trials and tribulations, the journey was immensely productive. A G was always alert to any idea which might improve efficiency. The journal is full of details of the construction of the butts, octaves, casks and other containers used for storing or transporting wines. In Jerez he warned that 'on my return I may have a proposition to make on the subject of corks that will enable us to grapple this long-talked of question — before we can do anything in the matter we want information and this can only be obtained by visiting the various producing districts'. Eighteen months later James Blyth and Charley Gold were duly despatched to make an exhaustive tour of Spain's cork-growing districts. In the office of their friend Manolo Gonzalez in Jerez, A G's ever-watchful eyes lighted on a 'hand lithographic press for striking off notices or circulars — it showed us that we do not make half use of lithography in our printing department.'

The journey not only led them to buy Loudenne; it also brought about the development of their export business.

In Malta they were cheered to find that 'it seems generally known that we do a large business and our name appears to inspire all with implicit confidence just the same as we look up to Rothschild or a Sassoon altho' we know nothing of them except that they are large'. Moreover, 'there does not appear any of that prejudice that we met with in England amongst those who happen not to deal with us and whose opinion is formed by us by the opinion of their own wine merchant or perhaps the channel we employ to distribute our goods — we feel sure therefore that if our Export trade is well done both as regards quality and putting it conveniently before customers that it will be at once responded to by all Englishmen abroad.' Although the party failed to find a suitable agent in Malta on the trip, one was found within 18 months in Trinidad, and before the end of the decade there were several in India. Even before that the Gilbeys had extended and reorganised their export warehouses to meet the increase in trade.

But corks, lithography, even potential export business, were only incidental to the main purposes of the journey — to visit Marsala, Jerez and Oporto, all three important sources of wine, but all displaying different purchasing techniques. In Marsala the Gilbeys were concerned to inject some competition into their supplier. In Jerez they relied on the advice of their great friend Manolo Gonzalez, and in Oporto they were content to play the field: 'not being engaged, married and done for with any particular house here it is difficult with so many admirers to keep on flirting and smiling at all comers', wrote A G. But by the time he left Marsala he had come up with a fourth system — a permanent presence in the producing district.

In Palermo, before setting off for Marsala, A G had a rare attack of nerves: old Ingham Whittaker, one of their suppliers, said, 'you will, of course, put up at our house in Marsala as there is no hotel worthy of the name — I felt myself in a faint voice saying "yes of course" — I was not thinking much about the accommodation — I had a kind of inward fear that we should never get there — They said the mail has now always a guard of soldiers, so that you need not be alarmed — I am not quite sure that this did not frighten me more than ever.' In the event the journey was uncomfortable, but not dangerous, and they arrived in fine form, ready to break up the cosiness they felt pervaded the only three houses which could supply the Gilbeys. 'We have done all we can', wrote A G from Marsala, 'to put them at loggerheads with each other and make future compacts impossible.'

Marsala is produced rather like port, the dry, rather harsh white table wine of the region strengthened with a mixture of grape brandy and 'must', unfermented grape juice, and heated, as Cyril Ray puts it in his *Wines of Italy,* until it has become 'thick and sweet, caramelly in colour, texture and flavour'. In the 1870s, the Gilbeys were buying enough marsala to fill half a million bottles, a twelfth of all the wine exported by the three main houses — Woodhouse (founded by a merchant of that name who had originally devised the mixture), Florio and Ingham Whitaker. Although the Gilbeys listed three varieties of marsala, they quickly came to the conclusion 'that provided the system of fortifying and sweetening is carried out and the proper

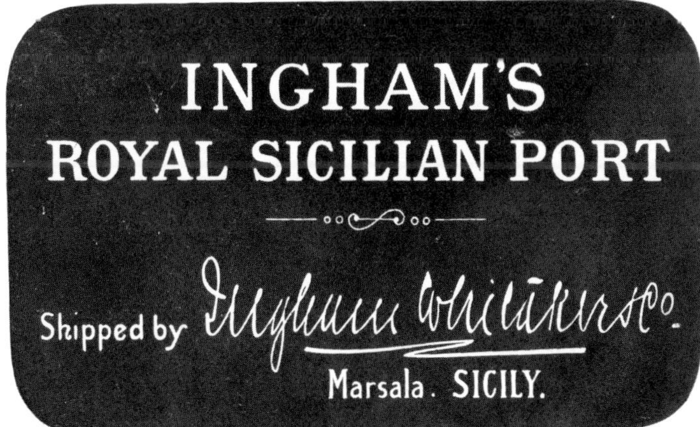

fining is used to reduce their reddish tint it appears impossible to show bad qualities in wines two and three years old, in fact there was scarcely a pin to choose between the various descriptions'.

This was bad news for the shippers: the Gilbeys' indifference to the quality of the wines they were buying greatly increased their power to fight the price rise the shippers were proposing (a major motive behind the Gilbeys' visit). Fortunately the Englishmen could divide and rule: 'As in Jerez and Oporto a certain feeling of jealously appears to exist and they therefore know nothing of each other's business with the exception of the quality of the wines each house ships . . . they are all under the impression that the other two have not acted fairly in the late rise but have continued supplying their customers at the old rate.'

The Gilbeys concentrated their efforts on Ingham Whittaker, their original supplier. Unfortunately they could never pin the whole family down in one place ('This single-handed fighting would exhaust a gladiator', wrote A G with pardonable exaggeration).

Eventually, in an epic encounter which illustrates the Gilbey technique to perfection, they got to grips with the old man. The 74-year-old Ingham Whittaker proved slippery. 'He made as many false starts as ever the starter had to contend with in the Derby', wrote A G. 'The old gentleman evidently with an idea of shirking the question took advantage of any remark we made to remember some story that had no bearing on the case whatsoever' — although the anecdotes were interesting enough for A G to repeat some of them — 'and when this failed generally succeeded by running off to his high for a pinch of snuff which took place at least fifty times during the interview'. Even when they got him partly he dived back to the good old days, which for him, as for his rivals, meant small shipments and large profits, the absolute opposite of the Gilbeys' commercial beliefs, which they had preached a thousand times in the previous days.

But the old man proved stubborn. Eventually, on the Gilbeys' last day in Sicily, he agreed it was absurd for them to pay commission to a London agency. This was the most profitable bottle-neck in the whole distribution system. One contemporary shipper earned £10,000 a year commission (equivalent to £200,000 or more today) while selling a mere thousand butts of sherry — less than half the Gilbeys' annual sales. Naturally the elimination of such greedy and unnecessary middlemen obsessed the Gilbeys.

Nevertheless, Ingham Wittaker was not going to retreat very far. 'After the deepest reflections', he had 'decided to offer us discount of 2 per cent on all our business . . . now as this concession was named after a very elaborate not to say prosy speech during which we had conjured up all sorts of liberal allowances we need hardly say that we were thoroughly disappointed when the figures at last came out'. The old man had hoped to do a deal on the spot, but the Gilbeys withdrew fuming, thinking it 'injudicious to make any further efforts now to get this ridiculous small discount increased' (later it was widened sufficiently for them to keep their business with the old man and sell his offerings at 1s 4d a bottle).

Unwittingly, Ingham Whittaker had finally convinced Alfred of the need to have a permanent presence nearer their suppliers. He concluded his account of their duel with the

old man with the prophetic words: 'We must have an establishment for ourselves in the wine-growing countries unless we can make arrangements that will give us the advantages we desire in purchasing and in this latter case we will forego the honor of being shippers.'

In all the countries from which they bought heavily they needed either the sort of 'establishment' they purchased next year at Loudenne, or a reliable local supplier. In Jerez they had put themselves into the hands of a man as remarkable as themselves, Manolo Gonzalez, founder of Gonzalez Byass. 'Don Manolo' had been building up his business for 40 years before the 1874 visit, the latest of many paid to someone they clearly regarded as a close family friend as well as a major supplier. They stayed with him, visited his racehorses, and went to the opera with him. He and his family were part of the clan: one of AG's sons, Newman, married a grandaughter of Manolo's, and 50 years after AG's visit two of his grand-daughters married Gonzalez boys. They were very fond of him, nicknamed him 'The King of Andalusia', spoke of 'his many admirable qualities, his knowledge of his business, his activity, his respect for other people's opinions, and an absence of any conceit about his own, and we came to conclusion that not only Spain, but any country, might be proud to own him'.

Yet they never loosened their grip. 'Jim in selecting our cheap wine marks finds it most difficult for all the lower grades are £1 or 30/- per butt dearer' than the price of similar wine from Gonzalez's rivals; 'the quality may be a little better but this is a serious rise'. The Gilbeys duly informed Gonzalez' buyers that they were 'allowing Mr. Gonzalez to be beaten by his neighbours'.

At Jerez they were among friends, and they were comfortable enough in Oporto, but their journey through war-torn Spain left them profoundly relieved at the prospect of returning to France: 'When we took tickets to Bordeaux', wrote A G wearily, 'we really began to feel that we were actually on our way home'. At the frontier 'the rain poured down — we did not care for we felt such a relief when we actually found our feet planted on French soil'. France for them spelt civilisation. They obviously felt at home there, and sent their daughters to school in Paris. On this occasion they were told that things were in a very unsettled state in France — 'if this be the case it is a pity they cannot see the countries that we have gone through the last eight weeks — after what we have seen elsewhere France to us appears a perfect Eden — what our old country will be like we cannot imagine'.

This map has been reproduced from 'The World Atlas of Wine' by kind permission of Hugh Johnson.

A LOVE MATCH

France felt almost like home to the Gilbeys, partly because they depended on French suppliers for some of their biggest and fastest growing lines, and thus visited its wine-growing regions more regularly than those of any other country. In the mid-1870s their sales of sherry were declining, and those of port merely stable: by contrast sales of brandies (mostly cognac) rose by more than a fifth to 3,200 dozen bottles a week within five years, and those of claret (and other light and sparkling wines) jumped by more than half to 2,200 dozen a week.

In many of the French producing districts the Gilbeys — like Marks & Spencer a century later — had relationships similar to, although not as close personally as, the intimacy they enjoyed with Manolo Gonzalez. In Champagne the Ayalas of Ay were 'trusties'; so were the Auberts of Ackermann Laurence, suppliers of champagne's cheaper rival, sparkling Saumur; so was Mr Hine of Cognac; and so too was a Cognac broker, Henry Rivière (both of whom married Gilbey girls). In Burgundy the Gilbeys' orders had been a major factor in enabling Louis Latour to start up in business on his own. He was one of those who had recognised early on that to get the Gilbey business you had to cut your margins and deal direct.

Bordeaux was the crux of their French business, however. It accounted for a high proportion of their purchases, and for the Gilbeys, as for so many other British wine-lovers through the ages, the wines of the Médoc set the standard by which all the others were judged. On their journey through Italy they often drank Médocain wines. In Naples they had noted that the native wine (Falernian from the foothills of Mount Vesuvius) 'retailed here at 1f 60 per bottle was appreciated by us very much. It was a species of full-bodied Médoc wine but there is still an amount of saccharin that would prevent it from ever showing its face in England'. And on their way through Turin they had been struck by a major new winery managed by a certain Mr Martini, who was especially proud of his 'celebrated white wine Vermuth' which he was surprised to hear that we had only heard of but never sold'. They eventually included his 'Vermuth' in their lists but were more interested in his red wine: 'the quality was such that it could hardly be distinguished from Médoc wines — the fermentation appeared much more complete, and the colour slightly less, than we should expect to see in so young a wine' — but in those far off days, Mr Martini's wine cost much more than its French equivalent. As Bordeaux grew more important to the Gilbeys, so the existing arrangements for buying its wines seemed less and less satisfactory.

Their business in the Médoc had always been in the hands of the Southards, Henry Parry Gilbey's former partners and close friends of the whole family. Alfred had even named his fourth son 'Southard' after Arthur Southard, the firm's London partner. Carver remembered him as 'a fine man rather stout with a ready smile and welcome in his broken English', and a regular visitor to Pantheon. The problem lay rather with his brother Henry in Bordeaux — like many such families, the Southards were based both in London, their principal market, and Bordeaux, which actually supplied the wines. He too was a friend: on their arrival in Bordeaux he 'came to the station to meet us, a perfect Captain Cuttle in a dress coat and white ducks', according to AG, recalling the amiable retired sea captain in *Dombey and Son.* Southard had busied himself before their arrival, making a number of recommendations (which they did not take) to use some of the full-bodied wines they had chosen for their 'A' claret to beef up the 'C'.

But their problem with the now elderly Henry Southard concerned more than mere questions of taste. 'We have had some very serious conversations with Southard as to the future', recorded AG just before they left Bordeaux, 'unless by some means he can be relieved from the severe strain that the business has at present on him, we shall discover or realise when it is too late that we have not been the friends to him that we ought to have been. His early training has not fitted him for carrying out the details of a large business and the result is he is always in a state of worry and excitement'.

The alternative was the sort of permanent presence envisaged by A G a few weeks earlier, after his indecisive encounter with Ingham Whittaker. Given the size and the complexity of the Gilbeys' requirements, a major investment was called for. Without a permanent base, they were faced with the unsatisfactory combination of an ailing Southard (he died a year later) and hurried visits which tested even their stamina. 'Having spent the whole of this day, from 10 o'clock in the morning to 9 o'clock at night, tasting these various wines, and having driven a distance of between 50 and 60 miles we found that we had made but very few purchases', A G had written wearily. 'It was therefore necessary that we should send a broker over the ground again to secure some of the best parcels on the best terms he could'.

They already had a broker, their friend George Merman, who had an office at Lesparre, the 'county town' of the Bas-Médoc. Like a number of his brother 'courtiers', he was a person of some consequence, owning Le Crock, a model estate; like his fellows, he played a crucial role as intermediary between the thousands of mainly small-scale growers and the handful of major merchants who purchased the bulk of the Médoc's production. Over the winter of 1874-75, the Gilbeys charged Merman and Southard with the task of finding an estate which would be suitable as the site for a warehouse and also as a supplier of wine in its own right. With the help of a friend of the Gilbeys, M Lalande, a leading merchant and proprietor of Château Brown-Cantenac, Southard came up with Loudenne*. AG and James Blyth had already tasted the estate's wines the previous year (they had found the 1872s 'very light in colour, but good breed'), and had noted that the then proprietor, Madame de Marcellus, was unwilling to sell her wine.

But clearly she was willing to sell her estate at a price, for the Médoc in the 1870s, like California's Napa Valley more recently, was a seller's market, and had become a fashionable place for outsiders to invest their surplus capital. In the previous 20 years, virtually every self-respecting Paris banker — the Pescatores, the Pereiras, and of course the Rothschilds — had purchased estates in the Médoc. Seven years before the Gilbeys came on the scene, the French Rothschilds had carried off Lafite, 'le premier des Premiers', against a syndicate of local merchants for a

*Southard's widow believed it was her husband who suggested this idea. The Lawton family, among Bordeaux's most distinguished, are equally positive that it was their ancestor M Lalande who guided the Gilbeys to Loudenne.

record 4,400,000 francs — £175,000 in 1875 terms. The year before the Gilbeys bought Loudenne, Château Beychevelle had gone (to a Paris banker) for 1,700,000 francs — a million francs more than Loudenne was to cost the Gilbeys. Loudenne's château and outbuildings had been valued for insurance purposes at 232,000 francs as recently as 1867, so they were paying less than 500,000 francs for the estate itself. Nor were they buying at the top of the market: the climax came at the end of the decade when Château Margaux went for 5,500,000 francs to yet another banker. So the Gilbeys were in good company — although, like everyone else who bought an estate during that deceptively profitable decade, they were destined to lose on their purchase for three-quarters of a century or more. The clan that had made such a fortune through its commercial originality was now to lose money by following the crowd.

Loudenne was not even a 'classed' growth, and had never been mentioned as an important estate. Historically it had been a mere dependancy of the much more important estate of Castillon, a couple of miles down-river from Loudenne. Castillon was a sombre, brooding fortress which had been one of the major redoubts of the Count of the same name, a leading Huguenot. To the profoundly Catholic French Kings, the Protestant Count was little better than a brigand, and after his defeat, the castle had been pulled down early in the 17th century. The two estates had then passed through a number of hands, until just before the French revolution, Loudenne was bought by a M Verthamon d'Ambloy, whose family managed to retain it throughout the revolutionary period, by no means an easy feat. By 1875 it was in the hands of one of his descendants, the romantically-named Marie Angélique Josephine Eudoxie, the widow of Viscount de Marcellus (a former soldier who had died 25 years earlier)*. Like so many other proprietors, she lived for most of the year in Bordeaux, and clearly had no reason to refuse an attractive offer for an estate which was sizeable enough, but whose importance had steadily diminished through the years — when the Gilbeys first saw the estate, only 60 out of its 470 acres were planted with vines.

Her family dominated the whole area around the small villages south east of Lesparre, with a dozen or more estates at St Seurin de Cadourne to the south of Loudenne, St Yzans de Médoc a mile or so inland, St Christoly and Begadan. Their wines were duly listed in Cocks and Feret (then as now Bordeaux's viticultural bible), but none were of great renown. Indeed, until very recently, the wines of the Médoc north of St Estèphe, five miles south of Loudenne, were dismissed as of little value or interest. The classic view was summed up by the late Warner Allen in his *Wines of France:* 'After Pauillac, St Estèphe is the only commune of Médoc claiming attention from the connoisseur; with St Estèphe this brief summary of the great wines of Médoc comes to its natural conclusion'. The Gilbeys knew this (the 1855 classification, which also stopped at St Estèphe, was then only 20 years old, and therefore unchallenged). The estate was obviously not being bought primarily for the wine it produced.

*According to the received account she was related to Châteaubriand, the celebrated French author. In fact the only connection was that her husband's brother had served as a young diplomat under Châteaubriand when the latter was French Ambassador in London in the 1820s. He became a disciple, acting as a sort of Boswell to Châteaubriand's Johnson.

The negotiating team which travelled to Bordeaux in April 1875 reflected the importance of the mission. Four partners — Walter and Alfred Gilbey, James Blyth and Ben Grinling — left Charing Cross Station at 7.45 pm on Monday 19th April, 1875. They arrived in Paris early next morning, with time for a bath and a substantial breakfast (beefsteak, chop and bacon) before catching an afternoon train to Bordeaux, where they arrived that evening 'in good condition to battle with various difficulties which Loudenne might bring about'.

One fundamental problem was how best to disengage from their old friend Southard. On the day they left London they had finally discussed the situation with his brother, and had telegraphed ahead to Henry: 'Picturing poor Southard very ill with the house filled with nurses and doctors, we telegraphed from Paris to say we were on our way and asked them to take apartments for us at the hotel' — an important gesture, because the Gilbeys were used to staying with their trusted foreign suppliers. In fact, as they discovered that evening when they went to see him, Southard was 'better than we expected to find him', indeed he 'was ready to greet us in his old style — in appearance he looks well and his muscular frame seems as well as ever'. Nevertheless, 'his speech dragged a little as if he had had a slight stroke'.

Because of Southard's illness, George Merman was usurping the role he had played for so long. 'Our visit somewhat excited him and he thought that George Merman had been a 'little childish' over Loudenne', reported Alfred nervously. 'In a matter of this kind you expect a little difference of opinion — no two men would go about it in the same way'.

Merman had clearly taken over the negotiations, and the resulting tensions emerged the next day when Merman and his partner Eugène Baguenard called: 'Loudenne was at once discussed — Southard took part — he had previously mentioned to us that if we purchased, he should like a notary that he knew to act for us — of course we had no objection whatever and mentioned it to Merman — he at once said that this was not possible, for he had, he considered, partly committed us, for most of the information he had obtained had been procured by a M La Chêne, a Notary now settled in Bordeaux, who used, previously, to reside at Lesparre and therefore knew all the district around Loudenne. Merman spotted him as a rising man and one particularly suited for our purpose. Of course this clinched the affair of the Notary should Loudenne be ours.' The Gilbeys knew enough of French rural life to realise that the notary, the universal adviser of peasants, bourgeois and aristocracy alike, was the crucial middleman, so it was unthinkable to abandon M La Chêne (even when the French railways were buying land on which to build their TGV — Train Grande Vitesse — in the late 1970s they were careful to placate the notaries on the route to facilitate the thousands of land transactions involved).

They had to refuse Southard's request; and before they left Bordeaux to inspect their potential purchase they had to face him with the logical consequence of their new policy: that they would, no longer be buying his 'Grande Marque' wine in large quantities as the basis for their cheaper clarets. Early on the Wednesday morning, 'after touching on Loudenne Jim very quietly took him on to the Grande

Marque and retailed to him the conversation we had with Arthur on Monday — he did not appear to be able to swallow it in one dose poor fellow'; so they repaired to the stores and made the best of a bad job by finding a use for some of the Grande Marque, which would improve their 'A' claret and 'at the same time relieve Southard of what we consider a weight so that if it is possible we shall endeavour to pull this off'*.

Obviously Southard was in no condition to accompany them on their 35-mile journey to Loudenne, but there was one relative of his on the trip, Edouard Brown, who was married to Mary Southard, and who had been chosen to manage the property. He joined what was by then quite a substantial party — the four Gilbey partners, two brokers and La Chêne the notary, on what Alfred called their 'expedition' that Thursday morning. Brown and the notary got out of the train at St Estèphe to act as an advance party, but the Gilbeys and their brokers went on to Lesparre to inspect some wines. They were in a romantic, almost lyrical, mood on what Alfred described as a nice spring day, although a little fresh for the Bordeaux weather. But 'the sun was cheerful and everything looking magnificent — everything so fresh and green except the vines which are only just bursting — the oxen were all engaged ploughing between the vines and all hands were busy in attending the vines, even the cocks and hens were playing their part in destroying the snails and insects'.

They were naturally tempted not only by the wines but also by the estate of Bessan, which they looked at between Lesparre and Loudenne. Château Bessan has now disappeared, parcelled up between other estates, but its full name of Bessan Ségur indicated its aristocratic origins: it was originally owned by the Ségur family, owners of Lafite, Latour and a dozen other estates in the Médoc in the 18th century. One of the family had married M de Verthamon, and in the 1870s it was in the hands of Odon de Verthamon, a relative of Loudenne's owner. Baguenard told them that M de Verthamon might be prepared to sell, and they loved it. 'One of the most compact properties in the district. . . . a brand much appreciated in Holland (it was termed the Château Lafite of Holland). The vineyards and property are in first rate order', enthused Alfred; 'they are this year planting more so that in the course of a few more years it will produce 200 tons, for even in its existing state it was much more productive than Loudenne'. And 'even though the buildings are in a bad state, a touch here would make them first rate'. The owner was asking 600,000 francs (£24,000) for this gem. Someone had bid £20,000 and the manager 'intimated that if this was again repeated he thought M de Verthamon might accept it'.

What with the excitement over Bessan and the lengthy tastings they had conducted, they did not arrive at Loudenne until 3 pm, tired and very hungry. They were obviously depressed, even though they found that another visitor was the Mayor of St Yzans, whose wines they had bought, 'the proprietor where Harry Gold lunched off dried Goose's legs and liver. Even the smile from this jolly old face did not cheer us up, for we were done up and had got that sinking feeling that Charley Gold always guards

*When the Gilbeys had the Diaries transcribed and typed they omitted everything about Southard, presumably because they wanted to perpetuate the impression that the operation had been more painless than in fact it had been.

against' — their only meal since breakfast had been a hurried picnic brought from Bordeaux. And even though they then breakfasted well — albeit rather belatedly — when they took their bearings of the property, their first impressions were mixed:

'We were disappointed with the interior of the château — even the fine trees forming the Avenue looked small and spindly, in fact we were a little sick at heart and had no "Heart for Mangles". However we surveyed the property. The situation is first rate and capable of great things, both commercially and artistically. The village of the Maréchale from half to three quarters of a mile distant is easily approachable by road, or by laying down a tramway. At this village there is a creek or landing place for small vessels to load and unload so that should we purchase, it will be a question of whether we shall build our Stores down by the creek or more convenient to the Château. To do this there is a field or two we should have to acquire, about which the Mayor says there will be no difficulty — we were glad to find that the river (we might say the sea for it is 10 to 12 miles across) was mostly used for all ships passing up and down to Bordeaux on the Loudenne side. The Channel or course of the river runs by Loudenne and any size of steamer can pass within a quarter of a mile of the Château. As a "Port" this makes the property very valuable. Between Loudenne and Maréchale is a favourite spot for vessels to "hove to" in bad weather. After taking our soundings, we surveyed the vineyards some of which are magnificently situated on

'We were disappointed with the interior of the château . . . After taking our soundings, we surveyed the vineyards . . . '

hills and gentle slopes. Brown considered them capable of great improvement. In one of the choice spots there are still 13 to 14 acres of white grapes which are used in making wines for the men and ought to have been rooted out years ago. In former times a good deal of common white wine was grown in the Bas Médoc. Besides this, there is plenty of ground where vines can be planted. We had another look at the Château. Whether we had pictured the interior a Margaux or not I do not know, but we were all disappointed. The furniture is not worth much but if it is taken away and the house dismantled, the interior would all require doing up.'

Characteristically they tasted a number of wines at St Estèphe on their way to their hotel at Pauillac, which they reached only at 9 pm. They then had a first-rate dinner, rounded off with a bottle of Delaforce '64, 'which would have graced the table of many a Monarch or even a Prince Metternich', but nothing was decided. 'We retired to bed', wrote Alfred, 'without coming to any determination about Loudenne'. They were called at 6 am and could not put off a decision any longer.

'We had settled amongst ourselves that when we got back to Bordeaux in the train, we would decide as to what we should do about Loudenne. We at first discussed the income and found that it would, as an investment, be a Glasgow (presumably shorthand for an unprofitable new store) for some years to come. We thought that if we married it to Bessan . . . that it would pay 5% on the investment. The majority of us came to the conclusion that if it was to be had for £20,000 it ought to be acquired if the purchase money was made easy. As we were not unanimous this was given up. The old conservative (Ben?) threatened to telegraph to the Governor. We then decided that we must somehow or other get a reduction in the price of Loudenne. At the same time we felt certain that it would be useless to offer them a less sum than the price fixed £28,000.'

In Bordeaux Merman had warned them that after they had seen the property their reply was to be merely 'Yes' or 'No' as far as the proprietors were concerned and that nothing less than the price given them of 700,000 francs would be taken. But in the train they came up with the idea of delaying the payments: '£8,000 down, £10,000 in five years and £10,000 in ten years bearing interest at 4 instead of 5. This gave us an advantage of £1,500. We explained it to Baguenard, who thought it feasible, so that we resolved that if it was to be merely "Yes" or "No" unless they agreed to the foregoing.'

When they reached Bordeaux they went over the ground with Southard — 'we felt very sorry that the dear old boy could not have been with us and given us the benefit of his views on the spot'. As part of the gentle letting-down process they agreed to take more of his 'Grande Marque' off his hands before returning to Merman's office that evening at 6. The Gilbeys got there a quarter of an hour early, but 'having just seen him go into the office we followed. He had seen the Marchioness Marcellus' two sons and they had fully discussed our offer and they were willing to accept it'.

There was more haggling to come. For one thing, 'the

furniture could not be included but they would verbally promise that the Marchioness would leave a good portion. They remarked that if we would leave it in this way, that they were certain we should not be disappointed' (in the event they were). 'Beyond that they could not ask their mother to go.' More important was the question of the terms: the Marcellus accepted the principle of staged payments but wanted half of the total in cash, payable on signature. The Gilbeys offered only £8,000. In the end they paid £9,000 in cash, another £5,000 within three years at five per cent interest, but payment of the remaining £14,000 was deferred for 10 years at an annual cost of only four per cent. Finally Merman emerged from his discussions with the Marchioness's sons, saying 'to two of his partners who were in with us "these gentlemen are the proprietors of Loudenne" '. The competition, they alleged, had been fierce: 'since the property had been under offer to Mr. Merman they had been offered the sum we had given for it without any stipulation'. They were to sign the contract the next afternoon but to keep quiet about it for the time being, because any publicity would have made it more difficult to buy the additional land they wanted.

Several problems remained. The first — the salary they were prepared to pay Edouard Brown — cropped up at dinner that evening: Arthur Southard had suggested £250 a year, but Brown wanted £400. 'This somewhat took the steam out of us and we nearly collapsed. We did not refer to it any more, that evening and slept over it — it however caused a little nightmare'.

The second problem only emerged the next day after the formal signing ceremony. The Gilbeys did not speak French, so 'George Merman's name had to be put in the deed as having interpreted it to us, and before signing it we had to write in English that it has been explained to us'. As a result an English version of the final deed has survived. It is written in Walter's bold hand and describes Loudenne as 'an estate or property called Château Loudenne situated in the Commune of St Yzans bas Médoc, Canton and Arrondissement of Lesparre, Gironde, consisting of the château, houses, stores, press house, barns, stables, coach house and other labourers and agricultural buildings, garden, park, warren, ornamental grounds, vineyard, arable lands, meadows and marshlands', which together with some outlying land added up to 470 acres. The Gilbeys paid an extra 17,600 francs (£700) for ten horses, 25 casks of wine, two cows, three pairs of oxen and a 'vehicle' valued at a mere £20. The Gilbeys were, however, graciously permitted to use the seller's name on the estate's wine for five years, although the owner promised to leave before the end of June.

That evening they dined at the old lady's, an occasion spoilt by a blazing row between Southard and La Chêne (whom the Gilbeys had come to trust). To save time and trouble the Gilbeys' notary was going to act for both parties, but Southard wanted his own notary to inspect the deed. 'Mr La Chêne said that it was impossible and if he Mr Southard wished it he would withdraw and wash his hands

Opposite: Loudenne set in perspective — seen merely as one arm of an international business, of which the nerve centre was the Pantheon.

GILBEY
DUBLIN
EDINBURGH
W. & A. GILBEY
PANTHEON
LONDON
CHATEAU LOUDENNE

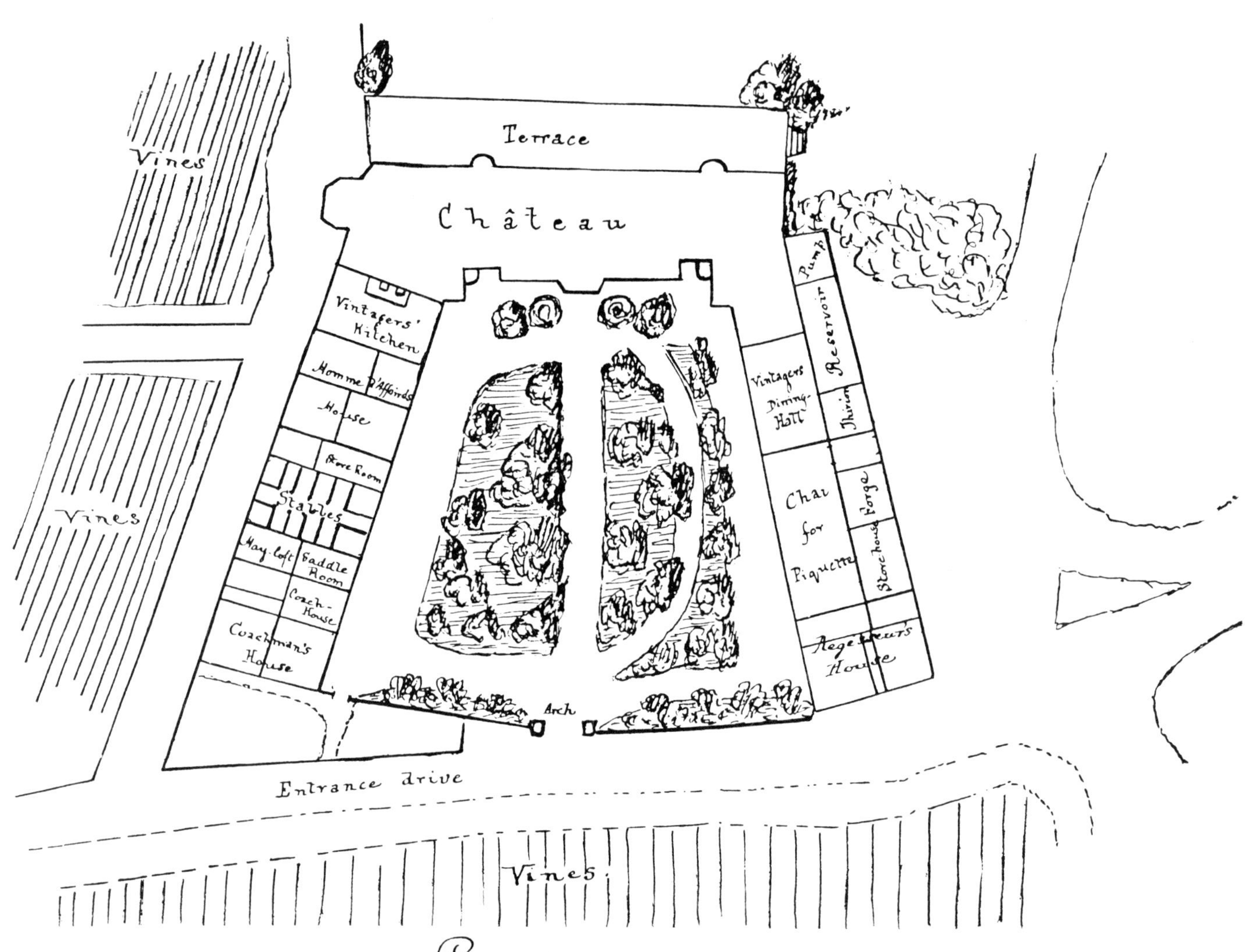

Plan of Château and Buildings attached. ~

of it. It was all Greek to us. Mr Brown quietly joined in the conversation, explanations which Southard considered satisfactory were given and the affair proceeded . . . and thus ended the first part of the Loudenne expedition.'

Once the Gilbeys had actually bought Loudenne, they were transformed, behaving, not like hard-headed businessmen, but like newly-weds with their first glimpse of domestic bliss. On the next day, when 'even the weather was everything that could be desired', gushed Alfred, 'our feelings on arriving at Loudenne were all that could be desired, and looking at it from the eye of proprietor, grower and agriculturalist and perhaps a little as we do in the light of a parcel of wines when they have become our property we felt more than pleased with our bargain. The situation on the Gironde stands far above most others — in the same way as Cliveden on the Thames. The slopes, the woods and Park-like appearance are very grand, and the house today is far beyond our first impression and this after coming from Château Crock is saying a good deal. The front elevation is very similar to the enclosed — it only wants a square tower or gabled roof up the middle and it would from the river, be a most imposing structure'. At this point Alfred sketched in the ground floor of the château, complete with terrace, and, inside, the long passage, the 'hall or vestibule' which still retains today its warm red tiled floor.* Then as now the 'drawing room' was the centre piece of the house, but in 1875 it was truncated, sandwiched between the three bedrooms at one end and a dining room at the other. Beyond the bedrooms lay a small chapel; the Marchioness 'had asked to be allowed to remove the Altar and furniture and of course we could not object'.

The party was not without spiritual refreshment, however: the Sunday on which they were inspecting the property was a very special one. On their way to Loudenne they had already met one procession headed by a priest, 'who had a most melodious voice and on enquiry we learned that it was the Sunday set aside for the benediction of the vines. It was a very pretty, simple and interesting sight. I noticed in the throng that all classes joined in the procession and some had decorations in their button holes.' At the château they were equally lucky: 'When we went down the Avenue on our way to survey the river frontage we were met by another procession with the priest of the village at the head. At the end of the Avenue there is a permanent cross, and today this was decked with flowers, and a temporary Altar placed by its side. It was very gratifying to know that they had come especially to bless the vines of Loudenne. The villagers here are a very intelligent looking class. The old Steward of Loudenne, who was shewing us round, joined in their prayers. He is a nice-looking old fellow and last year made 200 Hogsheads of wine of his own. There are nine families employed on the Loudenne estate.'

By then the whole party was elated: 'After we signed yesterday I told George Merman that £100,000 profit would not tempt us. Today I said that £200,000 would be refused'. There is little doubt that in the excited state of the

*When it was built, probably in the 1740s, Loudenne had been a pure 'chartreuse', so the salon extended the whole width of the house. The Verthamons had added the narrow entrance hall and passage; and whereas the loose limestone walls of the original château are now covered in pale-pink rendering, the 'new portion', built of more solid stone, is still the original grey.

Bordeaux market they did not pay over the odds for the property. While the Gilbeys were putting in their bid, the major merchant house of Nathaniel Johnston was offering 650,000 francs, and just before the party left Bordeaux Alfred records that 'La Chêne brought with him this morning a telegram he found when he got home from a gentleman at Lesparre to say he would give 700,000'.

Even in their euphoric mood they did not neglect business. 'We called at the little port of La Maréchale as we wanted Merman to see it. I was glad we did for the tide was out, and we could see the little creek at its worst. If it is practicable I am for running out a little pier direct in front of the Château, but on this point . . . we are somewhat divided . . . some of us thought that our stores would be better placed by the side of the creek at La Maréchale. I cannot go on with these for if any of us at anytime should be staying here, and have to walk for half or three quarters of a mile in the heat of the day, how often should he visit the stores? I want them in immediate proximity to the Château, so that I could put on a dressing gown and visit them before breakfast.'

Their only remaining worry concerned their poor friend Southard. 'The grief and the low spirits he shews at times makes us feel that his brain is not all in a healthy state', lamented A G. 'His stock is dreadful to contemplate . . . I assure you I have a sinking feeling in the stomach when I look into it . . . the fact of it is poor Southard has been entirely out of his depth the past five or six years. He is a dear worthy fellow, clever on very many points, but no more fit to take command of a business than I am to be Prime Minister.' But they still would not relieve him of all his — by now largely unsaleable — stock of wines. They merely impressed on Merman 'that if he wanted to see Southard better and at the same time do him a turn, he must not lose a chance of helping him out of his stock. He said the difficulties of finding an outlet were almost insurmountable.' Southard made matters worse when he angrily refused Merman's offer to take the rest of his obviously unsatisfactory 'Grande Marque' off his hands, albeit at a reduced price. Alfred did not in fact sympathise over much: 'The curious thing is that neither Southard nor Arthur or any of them seem to think anything of it. The fact of it is money matters are easy for them at Bordeaux — they therefore do not see or feel the pinch of holding such an immovable stock, the bulk of which is deteriorating rather than improving.'

They were on happier ground when discussing the future management of the estate. Alfred had proposed a sub-committee of partners, but added, 'When a thing wants constant and lasting attention it must be worked and fathered by a foster parent in the way that Charles Gold works for Glasgow, and Henry Blyth Dublin. As Ben has shewn such an aptitude for French we propose that he should take the position'.

This was logical enough, since Ben Grinling was in charge of the vast stores at Camden, of which Loudenne was, in theory, destined to be merely an extension. Alfred had already proposed — unavailingly as it turned out — that the estate's projected warehouses would also be used as a depot for their purchases of brandy from Cognac, less than 100 miles away.

Ben Grinling is generally thought of as the most

pedantic, bureaucratic of the founding brethren, but once abroad another side of him emerged, obviously to his partners' amusement. To start with he had been rather tiresomely uxorious. In Paris on their way to Loudenne, recorded Alfred, 'as distance from home appeared to have made Ben more loving he just had time to write a line to his better half — of course the remainder of our party had to follow suit' — normally 'better halves' do not get much of a mention in the Gilbeys' journals. Yet once in the Médoc he shewed himself surprisingly frisky. On their triumphal journey to Loudenne that Sunday 'Ben felt very cheery and offered to handle the ribbons . . . he took down a French horn that was hanging in the coach and woke up the neighbourhood, at the same time nearly bursting his old body but with as much confidence as if he had played one all his life'. He 'composed some verses on Loudenne, and is going to have them set to music on his return to London'. He was accused by Alfred of having an eye for the beautiful, spotting pretty girls in the day's processions. He suggested buying a yacht (to be called *The Castle,* naturally) which he would staff with a female crew; in Bordeaux, what with 'his tact and confidence', and his command of French, he made a 'regular sensation especially with the ladies'; and his reaction on seeing the processions that Sunday was to declare that 'if he adopted their country he should consider it an insult to them if he did not also at the same time adopt their religion'.

In the event, Ben was never given the individual power envisaged at the time, but on this trip he was referred to as 'General Grinling', although all four partners clearly felt entitled to give orders to Brown, 'much engaged' at one

'In the mid-1860s the clan was completed when their cousin, Henry Grinling (known as 'Ben'), resigned from the War Office to take charge of the firm's by-then-gigantic stores'. He was described by a contemporary as 'of the Civil Service type, great on statistics and would come to the board meeting armed with full details of bottles and cases sent out during the week'.

point 'in taking instructions from the various generals'.

They were as delighted with him as they were with Loudenne. The problem over his salary had soon been sorted out by Merman, so Alfred could report that Brown was highly delighted with the arrangement of £300 per annum and wine for his own table. 'By that point we felt free to discuss our various views with Mr Brown who expressed himself so nicely, without one particle of humbug about him, that we feel we have secured a man who will in every way watch our interests and represent us in the manner we should like. Knowing the laws, manners and customs of the country he will be most valuable . . . we are all very pleased with the sub-prefect and we explained to Mrs Brown that we hoped that they would make Loudenne their home, and feel as if they were the proprietors'. They were even more thrilled and impressed when they left: 'he got more attention at the Bordeaux station than ever I saw anyone before', wrote Alfred — he even got another carriage put on the train. And off they swept, via Champagne and their friend Mr Ayala, to send the first instalment of the Loudenne purchase price on their return to the Pantheon.

It was only after they had rounded off their estate by buying a couple of other parcels that the Gilbeys felt free to announce its purchase. At the end of June, they arranged for paragraphs to be inserted in *The Illustrated London News* and *The Daily Telegraph.*

The estate had been bought by the Gilbeys, went the announcement, 'principally with the object of establishing a vast depot where they can collect their extensive purchases of claret — the property being almost in the heart of the Médoc district — and ship them direct to England. By this means the charges incidental to the transmission of these wines up the river to Bordeaux and thence down the Gironde again will be saved and clarets delivered in London duty paid at a lower price than, owing to the heavy charge for railway carriage and the city octroi dues, they are procurable at Paris'.

The Gilbeys informed the French press that they too, might be interested in this important item of news. They also immediately circulated the relevant issue of the paper to all their agents, claiming that the publication of the paragraph 'in the chief columns of two such important papers as those above named shows the subject to be one of general interest to the public and we have no doubts that editors of local papers would in the majority of cases gladly copy the paragraph if their attention were called to it by a personal visit or a letter from you'. If the paragraph were reprinted 'it cannot fail to increase the demand for French wines in your district during the summer, while it will also explain to the public the exceptionally favourable position occupied by our Agents for supplying the Wines in question.'

Although the Gilbeys might explain the purchase of Loudenne as a logical business decision, yet, in the end, the motive had an element of social advancement about it. They were buying a mark of legitimacy, one not possessed by even the oldest-established and most reputable of their traditional rivals.

Pride in the purchase emerged only indirectly. James Blyth's second daughter, born in the summer of 1875, was duly christened Grace Loudenne Blyth.

THE MASTER-BUILDERS

Edouard Brown, the man the Gilbeys had left in charge of Loudenne, was no ordinary estate manager. He was a 65-year-old retired bureaucrat from a highly distinguished family of Bordeaux merchants; his surname testified to the mix of English blood usual in the town's haute bourgeoisie. Until early middle age he had, as a confidential report in the French official archives put it, 'lived very handsomely, devoting himself to the pleasures of the chase and fashionable life'. One of his brothers had married the daughter of the greatest of all merchants, Pierre-Francois Guestier. His own family had owned a classified growth, Brown-Cantenac, on the same ridge behind Margaux as the better known Brane-Cantenac. But then came a crash, the family's fortune, estimated at up to 12 million francs, was lost through a combination of improvidence and bad luck, and Edouard and his brothers had to earn their living, which in their station in life involved finding some form of official employment.

After three years as 'Conseiller' to prefects elsewhere in France, Brown was given his first independent post in 1853. He was appointed sub-prefect of Blaye, on the shore opposite Loudenne, but still in the department of Gironde. Although — like most of Bordeaux's merchant class — he and his wife were Protestants, and although he had, at least nominally supported Louis Philippe, the Orleanist King overthrown in the revolution of 1848, he became a trusted and highly valued official of Louis Napoleon, who ruled France as emperor for over 20 years, until 1870. When Napoleon III abdicated after the disasters of the Franco-Prussian war of 1870, every official of the Emperor's administration was relieved of his job. Brown had wanted to retire anyway, and in his time of trouble the 'Bordeaux network' came to his rescue in the form of Nathaniel Johnston, a leading merchant who was elected to the assembly in 1871 and who interceded on his behalf.

By the time the Gilbeys came on the scene Brown was in (probably badly-pensioned) retirement, an ideal man to carry out their instructions. Once they had returned to London these came thick and fast, in the form of detailed letters at least once, and sometimes twice a week. Astonishingly, letters posted on Tuesday afternoon in London would be waiting for Brown at the Post Office at St Estèphe, only a few miles from Loudenne, by Thursday morning. But the Gilbeys met their match in Brown. In reply to their courteous and detailed English, he sent prompt and punctilious replies in French. It is clear from the mass of correspondence preserved at Loudenne that, for the first year or eighteen months, they were testing out his suitability for inclusion in the prestigious band of 'trusties' — like the Carver family — on whom the Gilbeys so depended. Once he had come through with flying colours, they left him much more on his own (a pity for us, since the correspondence necessarily becomes less informative).

To start with they niggled over every detail. Their basic plan was clear: to establish their headquarters, complete with vast stores and a separate port, at Loudenne. Nevertheless, as Alfred wrote on his return from the purchasing trip, 'it was decided not to make any alteration of importance until after the next vintage'. The delay created considerable problems. As a result the positioning, design and construction of the new chais had to be crammed into a single year, since the new fermenting vats had to be ready to receive the 1876 vintage.

The summer of 1875 was devoted to the problems associated with the ownership of the estate and the château itself. From the beginning the Gilbeys were determined to transform the estate into a model agricultural property: all the partners had aspirations to land ownership (which Walter at least, was later able to satisfy in full measure), and Loudenne enabled them to indulge their combined passions for improvement to the full. 'While we are desirous of working the property on commercial principles', wrote Alfred to Brown shortly after the purchase, 'we are anxious that all matters should be so carried out as to make the estate a credit both to you and ourselves.'

Typically, their earliest concern was over the pictures required for publicity purposes. They immediately started badgering Brown in every letter to obtain a decent photograph of the château taken from the river — then the usual means of approach, and affording, then as now, the best view of the château. They were let down by a local photographer called Pedroni, and by 22nd May were back on to the subject: 'We have an opportunity offered us of getting a view of Château Loudenne inserted in the Illustrated London News . . . it is important that we should have this view without delay.' They got it in time for the issue of 4th September, but continued to pester Brown for other views for publicity purposes.

Characteristically, the Gilbeys tried to do everything at once. They were simultaneously buying horses for the 'omnibus' which conveyed visitors to and from St Estèphe station, changing the insurance policy on the château, worrying about the way the prices of barriques had risen. They were also trying to impose their own, very English, pattern onto every aspect of the life and work of the château and estate, and it was the clash of the two cultures over the following few years which created the Loudenne we know today.

The Gilbeys' first problem was with the estate workers. They were in a strong bargaining position throughout the Médoc because of the boom and the arrival of so many wealthy absentee landlords. As early as 13th June, Brown was writing, 'I have already mentioned the great difficulty which we are experiencing in getting reliable workers; this difficulty increasing all the time, not only at Loudenne, but throughout the region . . . On the news that Madame de Marcellus had sold the estate the manager and everyone working here made clear that they would leave' — although things had not been altogether happy before: 'It appears that this is not the first time that the estate workers at Loudenne had complained of being underpaid'. A few days later a relieved Brown wrote that he had managed to persuade the estate manager, at least, to stay, and that he would know about the others on 24th June, St John's Day, when by tradition, French agricultural workers gave in their notice — operative at Michaelmas, after the harvest.

The problem was compounded because the modern-minded Gilbeys had wanted to pay their employees purely in cash, rather than in the traditional mixture of cash and kind (usually wheat). Brown gave as one example the

Opposite: 'Valets' who tended the horses and oxen were paid 100 to 200 francs a year and 15 or 16 hectolitres of grain.

'valets' who tended the horses and the oxen on the estate. They were paid between 100 and 200 francs a year and 15 or 16 hectolitres of grain — and at harvest time, the harvesters were paid a set amount of grain for every 'journal'* they gathered in.

The Gilbeys did not like the system at all. In their view it was 'attended with decided disadvantages, and while it will of course be necessary that the various hands employed upon the property should be paid in accordance with the scale of wages prevailing in the district we think that payment should be entirely made in money, either at the rate of so much per day, or if possible, and which we should much prefer, on the piece-work system of a fixed rate for a certain quantity of each description of work performed. Of course this will not apply in the case of many kinds of labour but to take such an instance as mowing we think it would be more satisfactory to the men if they were paid at the rate of so much per acre as by that means the better class of hands would earn the higher rate of wages. Payments as at present either in whole or part in the shape of produce on the estate, are not only objectionable, but they are never estimated by the hands at their full value.'

That may have been true in Essex, but not in the Médoc. Eventually — as always happens when the new owner of an estate tries to alter age-old practices — the Gilbeys were persuaded that it was impossible to change the system. But — and again there are recent parallels — they would not listen to their own manager, but only to an outside expert. Sensibly, Brown consulted Theodore Skawinski of Château Laujac, a member of a remarkable family of Polish origin who managed many of the best Médocain estates in the 19th century, and who introduced effective remedies against many of the diseases which afflicted the vines of the Médoc. (Paul Skawinski was manager of Brown's old estate Brown Cantenac.) Theodore Skawinski shrewdly pointed out that if the workers at Loudenne were paid entirely in cash they would take the first opportunity to leave for a rival estate which paid partly in kind if the price of wheat ever rose above 25 francs a hectolitre, the value at which it was reckoned as a payment in lieu of wages. Come Michaelmas 1875, the Loudenne workers were re-engaged under the old system.

But the problems they posed rumbled on. At vintage time, a grave preoccupation for Brown was that the hordes of temporary harvesters who invaded the Médoc in September were suborned: 'In consequence of attempts made by the locals to corrupt them, they threatened to leave if I did not increase their wages'; which he duly had to do. In early January 1876 Brown agreed a rise of 50 francs a year to an estate worker who threatened to go and work for his father-in-law. The news spread fast and the other workers demanded the same treatment. In the event the original cause of the trouble left, but the news spread round the neighbourhood and produced a surge of applicants wanting to work for the Gilbeys. Later that month the coachman turned round and demanded to be paid entirely in cash, in a deal which effectively gave him a 20 per cent pay rise.

The Gilbeys soon worked out a proper policy for their French employees. In August 1876 they wrote: 'By pro-

*This was the amount of land one man could plough in a day ('jour'); the origin, too, of the English 'acre'.

viding good cottages and paying a rate of wages certainly equal to if not slightly in advance of the ordinary wages of the district we shall in course of time secure a permanent staff of good and efficient work people for the need of the property'.* By then Brown was taking the initiative, merely reporting back to the Gilbeys (albeit in considerable detail) and they went out of their way to back him up: 'We should wish you to feel that in all these matters we are content to be guided by your judgement and local knowledge of affairs'. By then, too, they had acquired Jean Bayle to help Brown supervise the property, and were advising ('We only throw this out as a suggestion') that he might combine the jobs of 'agent' and maître de chai.*

The Gilbeys soon worked out a proper policy for their French employees — good cottages and decent wages.

*They invariably had to pay more than neighbouring estates, because the soil at Loudenne was so heavy and difficult to work.

The cottages were duly built, and the Gilbey policy of enlightened paternalism proved generally acceptable in a countryside used, until quite recently, to feudal relationships. But the cottages were mere appendages to much more ambitious works.

The Gilbeys started with the château. Brown was as surprised as the Gilbeys at the way Madame de Marcellus had stripped the interior. The detailed inventory sent by Brown shows that the only furniture remaining was of the simplest, most rustic variety — a few rush-bottomed chairs scattered through the main rooms, side-boards and tables, all in a bad state, a kitchen stripped of all its utensils and containing only an oak table and a couple of white wood cupboards. The interior needed repairs to the value of nearly 3,000 francs, and the paving on the terrace would need another 625 francs. Brown also instructed the architect to round up some furniture, confining himself to the minimum required to make the château habitable.

Brown was soon recommending 'the best cabinet maker in Bordeaux' — the furniture could, he admitted, be bought cheaper, but it would be 'dits de Paris' — clearly a synonym for mass-produced items of dubious quality, the sort made for export, using cheap and unsatisfactory timber. By early July he was sending the Gilbeys a list of the bedrooms. The six on the ground floor of the core of the château 'could be considered as first class bedrooms, what we call in France master bedrooms'. Others were simply too small to

*In the Médoc every estate now has three senior people: the 'regisseur', the estate manager; 'maître de chai', responsible for the wine itself; and the 'chef de culture', in charge of the vines — a major task since there may be up to half a million individual vines on an estate. In the 19th century the 'homme d'affaires' combined general supervision with the role of 'chef de culture'.

be other than second-rate accommodation, although the only upstairs bedrooms in the little towers, were, then as now, amongst the most desirable in the château. Further away, in the 'corridor' — Brown used the English word — were other, even smaller rooms, suitable for the servants.

The Gilbeys were naturally anxious to stay in their château during their visit for the 1875 harvest; but because, as Brown explained, the workers were not used to the sort of work involved in repairing the château, they lacked the right tools, which caused delays. During the summer everything was being done at once: Brown was sending measurements of the size of the main windows in case the Gilbeys wanted curtains made up in England, and in the same letter warning of a further month's delay in the repairs because a large crack had been found in the wall of one of the towers, a problem uncovered only when the old wood panelling had been removed.

In the end the Browns were entrusted with most of the

buying. The lists were astonishingly detailed. Apart from the curtains ('Mrs Brown will perhaps kindly arrange for these'), the Gilbeys listed such diverse items as hat pegs, decanters, wine glasses, box for letters, dessert knives, a 'Chest for money', a set of harness ('the ordinary description of French harness with bells etc'), and a 'refrigerator'.

Despite the panic the château was in good enough shape by the end of September for the Gilbeys to stay there, thus establishing a regular pattern of bi-annual visits — in the

'Our feelings on arriving at Loudenne were all that could be desired. The situation on the Gironde stands far above most others — in the same way as Cliveden on the Thames'.

spring and at the time of the vendange — a pattern that was adopted for more than a generation. The first party was atypically small: the four partners who had formed the purchase party five months previously, together with Mr Miller and their great friend Paul Aubert from Saumur.

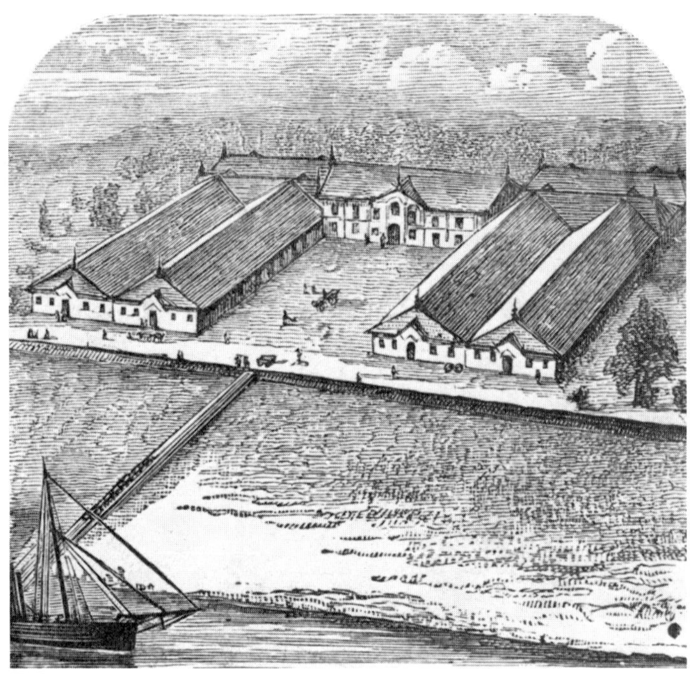

'By far the biggest single undertaking of the Gilbeys' at Loudenne, the new chais (left), and the new cuvier (opposite) cost the partners over half the price of the whole estate.

By then the plans were nearly complete for the construction of massive new chais. By far the biggest single undertaking of the Gilbeys, they were designed for the triple purpose of making and storing the estate's own wines, storing in cask and in bottle claret bought locally and shipping it all back to England.

Brown had found them an architect, Ernest Minvielle, described by him as the best in the area, who had already been entrusted with the repairs to the château and the purchase of the furniture. He had already built a red brick pile for M Lalande, who had bought Brown-Cantenac in 1860. (The Gilbeys liked Lalande's building: 'The château', they wrote following a visit in 1878, 'which has been about three years building, and the grounds, water-works etc., arranged by M Minvielle are delightful and well worth a visit.' To modern eyes it resembles a less stylish version of St Pancras Station.) More relevantly to the Gilbeys' needs, Minvielle had also designed cellars for many of the leading merchants in Bordeaux, and was the acknowledged expert on their construction.

The Gilbeys allowed neither Brown nor Minvielle to take a holiday that August. On the 10th the architect presented them with his plan, complete with approximate costings, even though their instructions to him had been rather vague (they were merely thinking in terms of stores for 5,000 hogsheads). Minvielle's scheme was a spacious hollow square, with 'a central building ten metres wide comprising behind the main facade offices, a private office, a tasting room, and the office for the maître de chai; to the left and right of this central pavilion six chais, three on each side, would be disposed around the central pavilion, three on each side.' All the chais were to be accessible from outside by means of gentle ramps, so that wines could be received from other châteaux. The new wines — both from Loudenne and from outside — could be stored in cask at floor level, and for that reason the chais had to be properly ventilated and aerated: 'Although they are specially designed for this purpose, yet they should be high enough so that casks can, if necessary, be stored there up to four high'. (Casks cannot be more than two high if they contain new wines so that they can be topped up and racked.) Work on this scale did not come cheap: the total estimate was a massive 330,000 francs, nearly half what the Gilbeys had paid for the property itself — and in the end the chais cost them 400,000 francs.

To soften the shock, Minvielle shrewdly appended a note to his estimate: allowing for the additional wine that could be stored in the 'first year chais' if they were used for older wines, it would, he claimed, cost his clients only 4 francs 85 centimes to house a cask for a year whereas it cost 8 francs 40 centimes to rent the same storage space in Bordeaux. Clearly his calculations depended on the proportion of new wine to be housed. By early September, Minvielle could confirm to Brown that 6,650 barriques — holding the equivalent of one and a half million bottles of wine — could be stored if the casks were piled up to the ceiling; he also demonstrated how the outside four chais could be arranged more flexibly to accommodate a mixture of older wines and new wines, either from the estate or bought from other owners immediately after fermentation, as was then usual.

Almost casually, the Gilbeys wrote that 'it is most important that these buildings be ready by the spring of next year'. They were in such a hurry that they had transferred to Loudenne the stocks previously held by George Merman as soon as they had bought the estate. During their visit in September they had visited the new chais at Couquèques and knew what to expect, but neither they — nor Minvielle, who had previously built chais only at Bordeaux

— fully appreciated the severe problems inevitably encountered with so ambitious a project, undertaken to such a tight schedule on a hill 40 miles north of the city, in a countryside entirely unused to works on such a scale.

The first intimation of trouble came in early October, when a sudden storm erupted over the estate before the vendange had been completed. The trees in the Grande Avenue suffered badly, and three horses which had been grazing in the fields near the river were nearly swept away by the floods.

The full extent of the problems first emerges at the end of November in a letter from Minvielle to Brown, in which he apologises for not having been able to receive him in his room, which had been 'so to speak transformed into a hospital'. He had been ill and 'Madame Minvielle had thought, doubtless out of sympathy, that she ought to copy me, with the one difference that at least I am up and about while she is still suffering rather badly.' He was hoping to start the construction work on 15th December, because the delay was clearly unfair to the contractors, but the problems were endless. Transport ('don't talk to me about it') was a nightmare; there was no lime ('they are not used to heating it for winter use — if only we could wait until the spring'); there was a certain amount of filler, but this was being reserved for the chais themselves (and in any case was different from the type they were used to in Bordeaux); and even work on the foundations was delayed (it was their luck that they had struck rock when digging them out). He had written to the mason and the carpenter at Loudenne ('two outstanding workers'): even they had not replied.

Minvielle struggled on, coping with intractable local conditions and asbsentee paymasters in London. They had clearly not grasped the need to differentiate the accommodation required for older wines, as Minvielle reminded them in a letter in January 1876, emphasising his previous experience and sending them the plans for the southern facade of the chais. The weather in the Médoc, he insisted, could get uncomfortably hot in summer, and the Gilbeys did not appreciate the need for insulation in such a climate. They had also not allowed for the need to store wines in bottles — so their architect rearranged the designs to allow up to half a million bottles to be stored, as well as an additional 1,600 casks. But there were still interminable problems over the height of the 'caves/chais'. The distinction was important. The Gilbeys were used either to the sort of cellars they possessed under Oxford Street, or to storage above ground. From Minvielle's rather exasperated replies to their letters (which have not survived) it seems they preferred underground caves to the semi-sunken chais more usual in the Médoc. And Minvielle needed an early decision in order to decide the level of the floor or the height of the roof.

The weather didn't help. The work was completely suspended during the first fortnight of 1876 because of ice and snow: Minvielle found the drive up to the château impassable and had to finish the journey on foot. At the end of January, he was to admit not only that the chais would not be ready in time, but that he had miscalculated

The new chais and caves were designed by Minvielle, 'the acknowledged expert on their construction'; they could house one and a half million bottles of wine at one time.

CAVES

the amount of brickwork required for the vaulted ceilings — an error which cost the Gilbeys another 2,200 francs. The muddles continued. Included in the new building was of course room for a set of vats — not all new, as Brown had hoped to rescue some of the existing ones. The Gilbeys had told Minvielle the size of cuvier they required but not the number of vats. This gap was not entirely their fault: they planned to expand the percentage of the estate planted with vines, and were in no position to forecast its virtual production with any precision. It was not until early March that Brown decided to have seven vats, two holding 10 tonneaux and five holding 15 tonneaux each, a total of 95 tonneaux* — far more than the estate's existing production. Even this was not enough for Minvielle, who finally insisted on a total capacity of 172 tonneaux, because the Gilbeys intended to plant vines even on the palus. Within 15 years he had been proved right.

Brown was obviously anxious to avoid any blame for the delays. In March he told the partners that he had 'already called the attention of M Minvielle and the contractor for the masonry work several times to the slow progress being made by the building works'. According to Minvielle, this particular problem resulted from a desperate shortage of masons in Bordeaux. Despite continuing bad weather, they hoped to be far enough advanced to allow the carpenter into at least one of the chais by the end of March.

Against these disappointments and delays, there was good news about the port, a key link in the transport chain. In March Brown wrote triumphantly of 'the possibility, I could even say the ease, with which a landing stage could be built directly opposite our new chais from which to load your wines' — previously the Gilbeys had been looking at an alternative scheme, whereby the wine would have to be manhandled the few hundred yards up river to the port of La Maréchale, which the Gilbeys didn't own. The discovery was caused by transport difficulties experienced by the master mason. The carpenter (a highly capable man, according to Brown) had built a landing stage directly below the chais which had stood up to the severe weather they were experiencing. Brown estimated that it would cost only 3000 francs to resolve 'the most important problem regarding the loading of wine from your new chais'. Sadly, in a note appended at the foot of the page Brown records that a sudden storm had severely damaged the temporary pier. Nevertheless, the carpenter remained confident that he could build a more durable structure. (Brown agreed partly because the water opposite Loudenne was a favourite spot for the ships to heave-to in bad weather, because it was relatively sheltered.)

The weather in March continued to be bad, but by May Brown was confident that they would be able to use one of the new chais, at least, before the end of the month, and could turn his attention to such relatively esoteric matters as the offical permissions required to establish a port — a procedure with which he was naturally familiar from his days as an offical at the port of Blaye. At the end of May, a large party arrived to inspect progress. In addition to the 'Loudenne Four' there were Mrs Alfred Gilbey, Henry Gold, Charles Ellis*, Charley Gilbey, Henry Parry's second

*A 'tonneau' is four times the size of a 'barrique' or cask: its contents fill approximately 96 dozen bottles.

*Probably a son of Alfred Ellis who had married Julia Gilbey.

son, who unfortunately died later that year, two of the Hines from Cognac, and Paul Aubert from Saumur, who had brought along his brother from Libourne. Although Minvielle had complained earlier that month that the carpenters had been working with the water up to their ankles, the visitors' book notes that the partners 'arranged for vats and scantling to be ordered for the cuvier. Plans and estimates to be furnished for a Port . . . Arranged with Architect to repair wells, alter Chapel, form a library, and to furnish additional plans for the future arrangement of the Estate'. By that time the château was more fully furnished. At the Gilbeys' express request Brown had found a clock which struck the half-hours, and in March proudly announced that he found that essential piece of furniture for any Victorian country house, a billiard table. The cost was a mere 850 francs, less than 1,000 francs for the clock. The table came complete with all fittings — and moreover, the seller would be paying all the transport costs.

Even though Minvielle was boasting at the end of June that they would be able to occupy the first chais early in July, we find him a few weeks later with a new excuse: a major public works programme to build new barracks had denuded the labour market of every type of construction worker, all seduced by the high pay offered by offical contractors — and when they weren't working for the government, they had been called up for their annual 28-day period of national service.

Nevertheless, on 19th August Brown was able to tell his masters that there was at least a roof over the new vat room. (He also had to admit that the first, airy estimate for the new port had been sadly inadequate. The cost had doubled to 16,500 francs — in the event it cost them over 27,000 plus another 2,500 for the little tramway which ran down from the chais.)

The vintage that year was late and the crop small, which was perhaps just as well, so that the Gilbeys were able to record that 'The vintage this year was the first made in the new cuvier' when they arrived on October 6th. Walter Gilbey, Ben Grinling and James and Henry Blyth had brought their wives along to inspect the new property. Another newcomer was their old friend and trusted supplier, Mr Ayala of Ay.

On their return to London at the end of the month, they wrote an immensely long letter to Brown, which effectively handed the property over to him under their supervision. (The next year one of their visitors paid him an unprecedented compliment when he wrote: 'Being reminded that I have not mentioned any "Grubs", all I have to say is that if Mr Brown becomes Commissariat General of the Russian Army, the Turks will have no chance'.) Despite their confidence in him, the Gilbeys' letter covered every possible detail, from the tramway — to be run up both sides of the chais — to the subscription the Gilbeys were prepared to pay to the hospital at Lesparre, the purchase of a mobile crane, and the sawdust to be placed over the roofs of the chais, 'so as to obtain an equal temperature throughout the year' (they had clearly learnt their lesson from Minvielle). They had asked him to design a house for the maître de chai to be built 'to the right approaching the château from the main road to correspond with the new cottages at present unfinished on the left side'. Within the château, the former chapel was to be secularised and turned into a library, complete with fireplace, and the bedroom next to the dining room was to be changed to a reading and writing room. Nor did they forget publicity: they ordered more photographs and sketches of the château, which they wanted within the month. They had also tackled the garden, ordering the wall to be demolished and replaced by a line of 'white wood posts with iron wire'.

By the end of 1876 the major works were finished, but they were perfectionists and later visits record a steady stream of smaller improvements. In May 1877 they 'discussed with the Architect the question of improving the buildings of the château, and making sundry additions in the way of house for coachman etc'. In October 1877 they 'spent day with M Desan discussing completion of Port, making tramway etc'. Early that year they had 'arranged with Mr Brown to commence shipping wines to London at the rate of about 100 hogsheads a month'. The pace soon quickened: between May and October that year, they noted 'about 2,500 hogshead had been shipped, all of which had to be carted to La Maréchale, the Port at Loudenne being at present only about half completed. Were struck with the quantity of earth removed and the importance of the works. The Chais and Cuvier all completed, and the principal things remaining to be done to give the finishing touches'.

In early 1880, Walter Gilbey ordered the final touches which completed the transformation of the estate into the property we know today. The visit was a melancholy one: it was first since the death of 'dear Alfred Gilbey', who had died in May 1880. As his brother wrote, 'his absence has been sadly felt not only on account of his sound business advice and good judgement but in his happy cheerful companionship which shows itself in every line of the "Diary of Visits to Loudenne" now in the library here and to the daily writing up of which he devoted many of the early morning hours. One and all feel indeed that his equal will never be known amongst his fellow workers.' After his death the 'diaries' and visitors' books preserved at Loudenne lose much of their flavour. For those nearer to him the memory was almost intolerably painful: it was not until May 1890 that Alfred's widow recorded her 'first visit to the château since . . . the year of 1879 when she accompanied her dear husband'.

Despite the sadness of the occasion, the ornaments Walter ordered through Minvielle were worthy of the great showman and ensured that Loudenne made an indelible impression even on the most casual of visitors or passers-by, whether they arrived by road or river. 'On the river frontage two columns fifteen feet high to mark the extreme boundary of the property. A shed at the Port to have on it "Château Loudenne W & A Gilbey" so as to be seen from the vessels passing up and down the river. Two towers on the top of each hill, north and south of the château. An arch at the south entrance of the château to face the high road. All these works to be carried out so that when viewed either from land or river they unite the different vineyards and buildings into "one harmonious whole".'

By then the tributes were beginning to flow. In October 1877, Hebert Hughes of Sheffield wrote that he esteemed 'the St Yzans District the most fortunate in having attracted to it so beneficial an influence as that of "La Maison Gilbey" ', and in the same page of the visitors' book came the ultimate accolade: 'Mr H P Gilbey, wife and daughters are leaving today after 17 days continuous enjoyment and they take back home with them a lasting impression of Loudenne and of the unceasing kindness of Mr and Mrs Brown'.

Two and a half years after his partners had bought the estate, 'The Guvn'r', on his first visit, had been conquered by the spirit of Loudenne.

The port, 'a key link in the transport chain'. Barrels were moved into the chais up a ramp. Then, as now, the view was 'dominated by the great black notice on the river wall'.

'A jointly-owned family house for working holidays'. Left to right from top in this 1898 house party: Lord Blyth, Mr Schlumberger, an unnamed visitor, Beatty Kingston, Bryans Ackland, Walter Gilbey, Arthur Gilbey, W B Tegetmeier, Mrs Alfred Gilbey, D Hine, W Gee, Sir Thomas Elliott, Alfred Gilbey, Gibbons Grinling.

AT HOME

Even before 'The Guvn'r' had paid his first visit, Loudenne had settled into the social role it was to play until the first decade of the present century — as yet another instrument of the firm's commercial policy. Of course the partners entertained their customers, suppliers, and other friends at the ever-hospitable lunch-room in the Pantheon, and on an even grander scale at their houses in London and their estates in the country. Loudenne fell somewhere between the two. Effectively, it was a jointly-owned family house for working holidays. Like so many others of its kind, it was accordingly neither pretentious nor expensively furnished.

The atmosphere of the château was well captured by one of the Gilbeys' more picturesque visitors, W Beatty Kingston. He had worked for *The Daily Telegraph* for a long time and was already a veteran foreign correspondent, having made his name during the Franco-Prussian war. He had subsequently written books — *Monarchs I Have Met* and *A Journalist's Jottings* among them — before he first visited Loudenne in 1889. Subsequently, Sir Walter Gilbey found him so useful as a propagandist for the firm that he came every year until his death 11 years later. His first impressions of Loudenne were vivid. He described the château as 'a long, turretted red-roofed building, for the most part one storey high, consisting of a ''corps de logis'', and two wings pierced by sixteen windows in a face fronting the river. It forms three sides of a quadrangle, containing several fine suites of apartments; the turrets abound in bedrooms, approached by tortuous flights of stone stairs; the old chapel in the corps de logis has been secularised, and is actually the biggest guest room in the house, with the former sacristy for a dressing-room. Between the long range of ''offices'' attached to the main building on its either rear flank — one containing the great dining-room and kitchen etc for the château proper, as well as a huge salle à manger and ball room for the vintagers, the other the kitchens, bakeries, the larders, specially affected to the commissariat of the labourers employed on the estate — are flower gardens and shrubberies, above which tower two magnificent magnolia-trees, well nigh as old as the château itself.'

The contents were workmanlike. An inventory dating from the 1890s lists few possessions of any consequence — strange at a time when Walter Gilbey was accumulating a remarkable collection of Stubbs' paintings at Elsenham, and when James Blyth's London house in Portland Place featured 'a removeable door between the dining room and the next room so that when he pleased he could double the size of the dining room and the number of his guests. The door did not part sideways, but sank into the floor'. By contrast, the single most valuable object at Loudenne was a Turkey carpet in the salon, valued at £60. Three more in the dining room added up to £50, and for the rest, only a Pleyel piano, three sofas, the famous billiard table, and an 'electric sonnerie with twelve buttons' were worth more than a few pounds. The whole contents were valued at little more than £1,000, while the house boasted only one bathroom at the service of a dozen or more guests.

Like other holiday homes, Loudenne was elastic in its ability to absorb large numbers of guests. As Beatty Kingston put it, in a piece of doggerel he penned after his first visit:

'Tis a picturesque, turreted, old-fashioned mansion,
Endowed with a generous gift of expansion,
Both the "Chapel of Ease"* and the "Batchelor's
Den"
Seems to stretch like a glove, down at Château
Loudenne.'

The list of guests for the first 30 years of the Gilbeys' occupation bears witness to the informality and unpretentiousness of the social scene. The visitors' book is dominated by the family. Walter Gilbey, James Blyth and Ben Grinling came regularly twice a year: just before World War I, James Blyth inspected the visitors' book and concluded that he had been to Loudenne 74 times in the 39 years since the purchase. To a varying extent they involved their families in the life of the château. Ben lived up to his reputation for uxoriousness and brought his wife on almost every visit after the first couple of years, while his son Gibbons, who first visited the château in 1884, when he was 20, came even more regularly than his mother. Walter's son, Henry Walter, started as a regular visitor, but his visits died away in the 1880s. Other members of the clan introduced to the estate their children in their early teens, and some of them caught the Loudenne habit to a greater or lesser extent. Only Charley Gold — who paid a single visit, and his numerous children, none of whom visited the château more than a couple of times, were entirely immune from its enchantment — even 'The Guvn'r' bought his offspring on what amounted to working holidays several times. And there are frequent references to daughters — Maud Ellen and Mabel Kate Gilbey, Kathleen and Beatrice Gold coming up to the château on their holidays from school in Paris.

Staying at Loudenne, was, in modern-day terminology, a partner's perk. In early 1886, Ben Grinling proposed that partners should be charged in proportion for the guests they bring. This, he suggested, would make them feel more comfortable. It didn't, and the subject didn't arise again.

Most of the non-family visitors were part of the extended 'Gilbey family'. There were suppliers, like Louis Latour, Paul Aubert, Mr Ayala, Mr Henkell, (supplier of sparkling German wine), the Hines, the Gonzalezes, and a number of their business friends from Oporto, like Francis Croft and Charles Wright of Crofts and Mr Warre of Silva and Cosens. There were a few rival merchants, a number of agents, and local friends from Essex. Initially the guests were allowed to write in the visitors' book. Apart from habitual eulogies, a few entries add something to our knowledge of Loudenne. A Mr R M Campbell noted how few butterflies there were to be seen: 'The Wall Admiral, Clouded Yellow and White appear just now to be the only species commonly found. Here and there are some good blues, coppers and skippers. The Clouded Yellow is much smaller than those which this year are so abundant in England.' And in April 1880 Henry Southard's widow, Louise, wrote a touching note on how her 'visit to

'Most of the non-family visitors were part of the extended "Gilbey family" ' — a typical gathering, mixing locals and family, on the terrace at Loudenne.

*The Gilbeys' transformed the chapel into a library. But by the time of Beatty Kingston's visit it had been split into a master bedroom (sometimes used as a kind of dormitory when the home was full) and a dressing room.

Loudenne gives a regret to the kind and sympathetic friend Alfred Gilbey, who is no more, and makes alive again the rememberance of ''him'' who first thought of ''Loudenne'' to be the happiness of his best friends the Gilbeys'. But Walter firmly excluded outsiders.

It was not surprising that many of the younger members of the family stopped coming to Loudenne once they grew up: until early in the century life there included a considerable amount of work. The work included the estate, endless tastings, and visits to the small number of châteaux like Le Crock and Laujac which were within an easy drive and also belonged to the family's small band of Médocain 'trusties'. And there were occasional day trips as far as Margaux in the southern Médoc, or by steamer to Royan across the estuary, returning via Lafite, Léoville Poyferré, Pontet Canet and other leading estates. But entries about the weather being 'favourable for long walks and getting about the property' give some idea of the relatively insular life led by the clan on their working holidays. Such an extended family felt no pressing need for outside social life. There were, quite simply, so many of them. In 1889, for instance, when 11 younger Blyths accompanied James, his wife and his sister-in-law, they felt no need for outsiders: 'The almost daily showers have not interfered with our outdoor exercises', wrote Walter Gilbey on that occasion, 'the game of cricket having taken place for fully three or four hours daily during the whole time we have been here. . . . the whole stay was pleasant and healthful' — just the sort of peaceful family holiday avoided by older children.

The high spot of the year was of course the vintage itself, and the vintagers' ball which provided its climax. To this day the best description remains that of Somerville and Ross, who visited the estate during the vendange in 1891, on a tour of the Médoc on behalf of *The Lady's Pictorial.* In the absence of the Gilbeys, Paul Aubert (whom they referred to as Mr A) looked after them. They were whisked the seven miles from the station in a smart English omnibus. On arrival they were shown into 'a large drawing-room, with windows opening onto an old stone terrace, beyond which were brilliant flower beds, and, in the distance, a blue strip of river; afternoon tea of the English kind stood ready, with a pile of letters and papers waiting beside it; a billiard room opened on one side, a library on the other, all empty, and luxuriously expectant of our occupation.' Then they moved among the vines to 'watch the sign that was now so familiar and yet always so fresh, the women's figures moving waist-high in the green — the men carrying the heavy hottes of fruit on their necks, the overseer with his eight-foot pole pointing faithfully to the bunch of grapes left behind by the careless vendangeuses, the hurry and bustle of everything, and the creamy oxen stepping slowly and imperturbably through it all, with their seventeen hands of height shrouded in grey draperies to preserve them from the flies'.

Beatty Kingston was more practical, providing an exact description of the gathering of the grapes and their transport to the 'cuvier or press-house. . . a rectangular building about 150 feet long and 30 foot deep, pierced in front on its upper floor by three large openings, behind each of which is a large circular wine-press, placed exactly above a 200 gallon vat on the ground floor. A crane lifted

The harvest: left, 'the creamy oxen stepping slowly and imperturbably'; above, a vendangeuse, her basket laden with grapes; and below, the 'men stationed in the pressoir'.

the load and tipped it into the wine press. Men stationed in the pressoir — not barefoot as of yore but shod with clean wooden shoes — convey the grapes with scoop-sided shovels to the égrappoir, a machine by which the fruit is squeezed and separated from its stalks. It is then pressed and the juice — resembling diluted bullock's blood in colour and consistency — that flows freely from it, is carried into the vat below by a trough traversing the lower edge of the pressoir'. Beatty Kingston, ever the propagandist, described how the grapes 'are mechanically assisted to make themselves into wine' — thus spreading the Gilbey gospel that claret was a pure natural beverage.

Somerville and Ross agreed with the calculation 'that the vintagers on this estate eat during the vintage an amount of grapes equal to a hogshead of claret — a creditable performance for people who are forbidden to eat any and are under constant strict surveillance. "We cannot enforce the rule" said Monsieur A, beckoning to us two girls from the end of a row; "we can only prove when it is broken. Put out your tongues!".

'This direction was to the two grinning vendangeuses; and in response two large tongues, as purple-black as a parrot's, were presented to us, while the eyes of their owners goggled above them with guilty deprecation and an inextinguishable sense of the absurdity of the situation. They had the full sympathy of the jury, and the judge only held up his hands and laughed too.'

Left: Vintagers ready for work — 'the overseer with his eight-foot pole' is on the left. Opposite: 'The harvesters ate extremely well' in the vintage kitchen.

Like a good journalist, Beatty Kingston found that the harvesters ate extremely well. Attracted by the delicious smell, he penetrated into the kitchen used to feed them, equipped with 'huge brick ranges heated by odiferous sarments*'. The soup comprised 'prime ribs of beef, carrots, onions, potatoes, cabbages in profusion, and two or three heads of garlic: any number of thin slices of well-baked bread; a sprinkling of salt, and a few capiscum shreds'. He promptly arranged to be fed with this delicious brew at the château itself. The estate's accounts prove that his description was no exaggeration. During the 1900 vintage, the harvesters consumed 15 hundred-weight of meat (as well as over two hundred-weight of cod fish), quantities of oil, garlic and onions, 876 loaves and eight sacks of potatoes.

*Vine prunings

A guest taking a stroll along the walk dominated by the red brick arch built by Walter Gilbey.

The high point of the harvest was the vintage ball, an event normally attended by the family and its guests, who in 1891 were worthily represented by the Auberts and Somerville and Ross. The dance was held in the vintage kitchen, a room 'with a musicians' gallery running across one end of it — an accessory that showed that dancing was as recognised a part of the programme as dinner'.

A deputation came to present a bouquet to the hosts from the château (one year a small party trooped up to the château and presented a long poem 'read with much feeling by Léonie Fauchey, age 14, the youngest girl of the party'. It was duly paraphrased by the ever-obliging Beatty Kingston, and terrible stuff it is too, full of references to 'lithesome dark-eyed girls' seen by a 'swallow young and fleet', asking 'what is preparing in the mansion fair of our good masters' — though, in justice, it is difficult to imagine a party of Victorian hop-pickers coming up with a poem of any sort!).

When Somerville and Ross attended the ball, they were soon swept off their feet in the contre danse, 'a sort of Kitchen Lancers'. It was pretty strenuous, 'and the only balm in Gilead was the sight of Madame A cleaving the floor of dancers in the arms of a little creature whom I took for a stout child of ten years old, till I subsequently saw his moustache'. By the end the two ladies were 'sorry spectacles . . . we should have been even still more dilapidated had it not been for those intervals wherein we were talked to by our respective vine-dressers as agreeably, as politely, and with as easy a selection of topics as if they were daily in the habit of discoursing to English ladies'. The two were Anglo-Irish rather than English, and noted with surprise and approval that 'not once during our fortnight in the Médoc did we see any man who had taken more than was good for him'.

This picture of rustic bliss was occasionally interupted by larger and more important groups of visitors. The first was in October 1889, when two separate parties, one of 23, the second of 19, visitors descended on the château (among them Beatty Kingston, on his first visit).

They included all the partners and their wives (with the notable exceptions of the Gold brothers). The first party boasted six members of the Council of the Royal Agricultural Society of England — one of Walter's major interests. They had been visiting the Paris Exhibition — which had featured a prize-winning model of the estate. They travelled by a specially chartered steamer, and toured the Médoc down as far as Brown-Cantenac, where 'they were most hospitably entertained by Monsieur Lalande'.

Walter Gilbey's personality is firmly imprinted on the visitors' book for the quarter of a century between his brother's death in 1879 and his last visit in 1904, and it reflects his passionate interest with the agricultural, rather than the social, side of life at the château. Apart from his endless arguments about digging and trenching, he was fascinated by every detail of the vintage. On his last visit he noted how 'in most years, from 13 to 14 small bunches of grapes can be counted from an average of vines. This spring it is easy to count on a vine, taken from an average number of vines, from 16 to 17 small bunches'.

He noted the temperature every day, and less scientifically, measured the overall weather by the need for fires in the rooms. Loudenne was always a chilly house, and

Holidays during the long Edwardian summer at Loudenne tended to be 'pleasant and healthful' rather than eventful.

Visit – Vintage 1900.

Name	Place	Left	Remarks
Sir Walter Gilbey Bart	London	Left 3rd Oct	Arrived Sunday morning 23rd September – Left Charing Cross 10 o'clock Saturday, coming right through via Paris. Bordeaux to St Estèphe station.
Mr Ralph Palmer	— do —	3rd Oct	
" Christopher W. Wilson	Rigmaden Park Westmorland	3rd Oct	
" W. B. Tegetmeier	London	3rd Oct	
" W. Beatty Kingston	— do —		Mr Kingston left 30th Sept being seriously ill to return by "Albatross". His family are to blame in allowing him to leave home and his medical adviser must have known that his condition was critical.. In the journey by railway and boat several times he gasped for breath and it was thought he would die.–
Sir James Blyth Bart	— do —	Left 2nd Oct	Arrived Monday morning 24th September, – Came via Paris – Bordeaux and thence by steamer to La Maréchale.
Mr Henry Blyth	— do —	30th Sept	
" Jack Barrow	— do —	2nd Oct	
" Carl Bogler	— do —	30th Sept	
" Garrett Taylor	Norwich	30th Sept	
" Henry Brown	Leeds	30th Sept	
" Paul Aubert	Saumur	1st Oct	Arrived Monday afternoon, 24th September, at St Estèphe Station.
" Frédéric de Luze	Saumur	26th Sept	
Sir Charles Howard	London	2nd Oct	Arrived Thursday evening 27th Septbr by Railway
Mr A. Sanderson	Western Australia		Still staying at the Château – His visit here, since February is to learn viticulture in the Médoc and to improve himself in French.
Mr Norman Gilbey	London.	Left 2nd Oct	Arrived on Sunday 30th September, from St Estèphe station.

the Gilbeys had installed small, but extremely efficient fireplaces (complete with cast-iron mouldings of galloping stallions) in the principal rooms. The occasions when fires were not needed in May or at the end of September were rare and thus worthy of notice. For all the eccentricity of some of Walter Gilbey's ideas, many others were astonishingly modern. As early as 1883, he was trying to separate out the different grape varieties in the fermenting vats, 'whereas hitherto the grapes from two or more descriptions of vines such as the Merlot and the Malbec have been employed in the same vat. It will be interesting to see the result of employing one kind of grape, and simply allowing the fruit to pass into the vat without the juice from the stalks. This idea of not admitting the juice pressed from the stalks to pass into the vat with the fruit was suggested by Sir T Spencer Wells' — an eminent surgeon and close friend of the family.

Walter Gilbey also recorded the deaths of his partners, coming as they did shortly before his own retirement from the Loudenne scene, and these brief death notices marked the end of an era. They also provided a guide to his real feelings about his partners. Henry Gold, who died on 23rd May 1900, was 'my dear brother-in-law', whose 'genial and amiable presence will ever be remembered with feelings of regret by those who knew him'. By contrast Henry Arthur Blyth, who died in January 1901, merely 'has many friends to mourn his loss'.

Even worse befell the wretched Beatty Kingston. It is easy to make mock of him. His poems were terrible*, and in many ways he was merely one of the clan's innumerable hangers-on (the partners, albeit with some misgivings, allowed him £20 in travelling expenses for his annual visits to Loudenne). Yet, as the quotes from his books and articles show, he was a serious observer, who provided the sort of invaluable details omitted by more distinguished literary figures. He deserved better than the curt and irritable note written after he had died on the return journey from the vintage visit in 1900: 'Mr Kingston left Sept 30th being seriously ill to return by the 'Albatross'. His family are to blame in allowing him to leave home and his medical adviser must have known that his condition was critical. In the journey by rail and boat several times he gasped for breath and it was thought he would die.'

The journey by boat and rail was the normal route to Loudenne. The Gilbeys tended to be creatures of habit. In 1913 Lord Blyth recorded how it was the 50th anniversary of his first trip to Paris with Alfred Gilbey, and how, 'although not a single year has passed since that date without having been many times to Paris, yet I have always stayed until this visit at the Grand Hotel'. The routine for the Loudenne visits had been established on their very first journey: the afternoon boat train from Charing Cross, an early morning arrival in Paris, breakfast and a bath, then train either to Libourne or to Bordeaux — '9 hours, an exceptionally good performance by a French express' — thence by steamer, sometimes specially hired if the party was big enough, to La Maréchale. By 1889 they had adopted an alternative arrangement. Morning boat train to

*Although I must confess to a guilty fondness for one verse:

> I have strolled through the purlieux of famous Lafite,
> And the Rothschilds, I fancy, must take a back seat
> In the ranks of Médoc viticulturalists, when
> Compared with the Gilbeys of Château Loudenne.

Paris, and then an overnight train, a journey 'comfortably performed, in two lit toilette compartments, warmed by a new system of pipes from an outside stove, but the windows of the carriage were covered with ice'. In August of the same year the journey 'was accomplished comfortably and without fatigue' in a record 26 hours door to door, 'thanks to the complete arrangements having been made beforehand through Cooks' people in London'.

Less hurried visitors could take one of the regular steamers which plied betwen British ports and the Gironde, the 'Pacific Mail Steamer Illemani from Liverpool' or 'Royan Steamer . . . by way of Jersey, St Malo, Redon and Royan'. In 1893 Sir Walter Gilbey and a few friends boarded the 'Hirondelle' at London, on Friday midday and arrived at Pauillac early Monday morning. 'A splendid passage, fine and warm and the sea like a lake the entire journey' (on the short journey across the estuary from Royan the following year 'the river was rough and caused some of our French friends discomfiture, particularly Mr Paul Aubert, whose complexion became livid'). Nevertheless, the journey, like the visits themselves, varied very little during the first 25 years of the Gilbeys' ownership.

NEW BROOMS

It was easy enough for the Gilbeys to extend to Loudenne the sort of social life they enjoyed in England — if only because they were surrounded by foreign friends wherever they were. When it came to running Loudenne as a vineyard, their major problem was their airy assumption that they could impose on the Médoc the agricultural methods and habits employed in their native Essex. Sometimes they succeeded, but often they failed, and their attempts invariably met resistance from the locals.

Their first problem was with Daille, the métayer, the tenant who farmed half of the 200 acres of the estate furthest from the river beyond the main north-south road. As was usual at the time, he was a sharecropper, and indeed the Gilbeys actually owned the cattle which grazed on the land he leased. The arrangement was never going to be overly profitable for the landlord, so the Gilbeys' first instinct was not to renew the lease and to farm the land themselves. But Brown warned against this step. No, the rent was not high, but 'at least you can rest assured that these lands are well maintained. In any case this land could not be added to those cultivated by the estate's own work force at the moment, on account of the great difficulty we are having in finding workers. So I do not hesitate to advise you to keep the métayer for a year longer. We will then have the time to examine the best future policy.' The Gilbeys agreed, but only for the year to Michaelmas 1876: 'At the end of that period, however, we have no doubt we shall prefer taking the property into our own hands'.

It did not happen. At Easter 1880 the partners reported, after a tour of inspection of the lands the other side of the road, that 'this portion of the estate is divided into about 102 acres, part pasture part corn etc and about 101 acres forming the métairie, the latter worked by Daille at present on a monthly lease. The last season here had been a very unfavourable one, extremely wet and cold. Notwithstanding, there were evident improvements since our previous visit, and with time and opportunity the same improvements will doubtless continue to show themselves to a very marked extent in the vine lands, the great obstacles to any immediate and general change are to be found in the difficulty of finding labour and the lodging of same when found.' The seven new cottages had not been enough to cover the estate's requirements, and within a few years they were to build 20 more.

But the Gilbeys still had great plans for the outlying farmlands: once 'good water' was available from the well near the château, 'steps would have to be taken for improving and adding to the existing farm buildings, with a view ultimately to the breeding and rearing of cattle for the working and use of the estate'. In the end Daille had to be included in these plans: in the mid-1880s we find him borrowing 4,000 francs from the Gilbeys to buy the new cattle, and arguing that because the Gilbeys were joint owners of the beasts, he should pay only 2½ per cent interest, half the proper rate. Even then he did not pay the reduced sums.

In the 1890s Daille was still there, recording how he had first been granted a lease back in 1856, and claiming that he would repay, not only the 4,000 francs he had borrowed from the Gilbeys, but even the 4,000 he had originally borrowed from their predecessor, Madame de Marcellus. Things did not improve in practice either. In April 1894

they 'had two interviews with Monsieur Daille to explain to him our desire to establish an altered system in working the farm (the métairie). We expressed a wish to take over the farm and work it ourselves under his management. We gathered from the conversation that he was doing no good for himself under the present system, and that he required an additional £80 to the £320 which already stands to the debit of the Métairie account. Mr Daille is to consider our proposals and write us thereon.'

The letter must have been persuasive. Six years later, in January 1900, the partners noted that the profit received the previous year amounted to a mere £62 3s 6d, the smallest since 1893. Even so, 'considering the number of years Daille has held his position of métayer, we do not think it advisable to institute any change for the present. However when a change is to be made it will be necessary to reconsider the system of working the Métairie farms'. Later that year things had got worse and they finally plucked up their courage: 'From the unsatisfactory way the rent has hitherto been paid by Daille, it is now decided to get possession of his farm, and instructions were given accordingly'. His eventual eviction seems to have been

It took the Gilbeys 'only a few years to institute probably their single most revolutionary step, the introduction of horses instead of the oxen used to plough the vineyards from time immemorial'. But, although horses were used for many jobs, Walter Gilbey never managed to dispense with the oxen entirely.

amicable enough. In 1910 the partners 'paid Daille a visit at his farm', so clearly they kept up with him. But the point had been made: there is still a métairie, its land leased to a local farmer.

It took the Gilbeys a quarter of a century to get rid of a single tenant, but it took them only a few years to institute probably their single most revolutionary step, the introduction of horses instead of the oxen used to plough the vineyards from time immemorial. The step was inevitable, given the role played by Walter, in particular, in championing the cause of the British shire horse. As he said, 'large shire horses were never used before in vineyards in the Médoc in the place of oxen. It may be said that each horse takes the place of two oxen and performs the work much quicker, compelling the ploughman to be more active in his work.' The pioneers were Russell and Edgeware, imported (presumably by boat direct to La Maréchale) in 1880, followed two years later by four more — Elephant, Giant, Spencer and Jonas. By the next year Walter was reporting home that 'the six shire horses sent from England are doing hard work, reflecting credit on Mr Brown and those who have had them under their charge. The first two, sent out about three years ago, are in blooming health, walk sound and free. The four sent out last year have been doing the hard work on the estate regularly, and considering the heavy state of the land from the continued wet weather and spring up to the end of June, they are looking remarkably healthy and well. They are perhaps not so acclimatised as the two horses sent out first, but this could not be expected.'

Encouraged by this experiment, the shire horses were joined in 1885 by three light horses, 'vanners' — Royston, Coll and Georgette — who, with Lightsome and Nimble, shipped out in 1888, 'did regular work on the estate and also do what is required in the way of station work, carriage work etc.' The first sign of trouble came in 1890 when Walter reported that 'the gelding white hack was sent back to our Camden stables as he did not take kindly to Loudenne'. But, by the next year, a dozen horses were working on the estate (including the apparently effective stallion, Gay Wonder, who arrived in 1887), and all were in 'good working condition, which is much to be satisfied with considering six out of ten of the heavy ones were sent from England nine and eleven years ago'.

By then Walter Gilbey had been forced to admit that his beloved English shire horses could not completely replace the bullocks. 'There are four pairs of working bullocks in addition to the horses', he wrote; 'these animals are indispensable for work in the vineyards on the hills, and there is much work on the estate for which they are most useful' — although to the end he classed them as honorary horses. In 1900 he reported that 'all the horses, including the working bullocks, are healthy and in good condition'.

Ten years earlier Somerville and Ross had recorded: 'There is a stable full of great English cart-horses at Loudenne, such as had not been seen in France since the days of Agincourt, but these descendants of the medieval warhorse are used only for the rougher farm-work; it is said that the oxen, from their clockwork slowness and placidity, do not break or injure the vines as a horse might, and, though this is contradicted, and the days of oxen are said to be numbered in the Médoc, they still pace in couples from vineyard to cuvier, setting their hoofs down together with the grave accuracy of a minuet, neither slackening nor straining, whether the two tall tubs on the cart behind them are full or empty'. In the event, the days of oxen in the Médoc were numbered in thousands, for they survived until finally replaced by the tractor only a few years ago.

The build-up of animals on the estate created other problems: 'The question of the hay supply becomes of great importance, and on that account we decided during the visit to abandon a proposed exchange of some fifty acres of meadowland adjoining St Yzans for communal land . . . the hay to be supplemented by . . . five acres of beetroot to be grown annually on the métairie lands'. From 1890 on they kept regular detailed reports on the state and size of the hay crop.

But beetroot, hay and bullocks were mere accessories to the vines and the wine they produced. The Gilbeys did not start replanting the vineyard immediately — the chais came first — but they did something more revolutionary. As far

Another Gilbey revolution — 'from the moment they bought the estate the fields were to be indentified by numbers'.

PLAN OF ESTATE

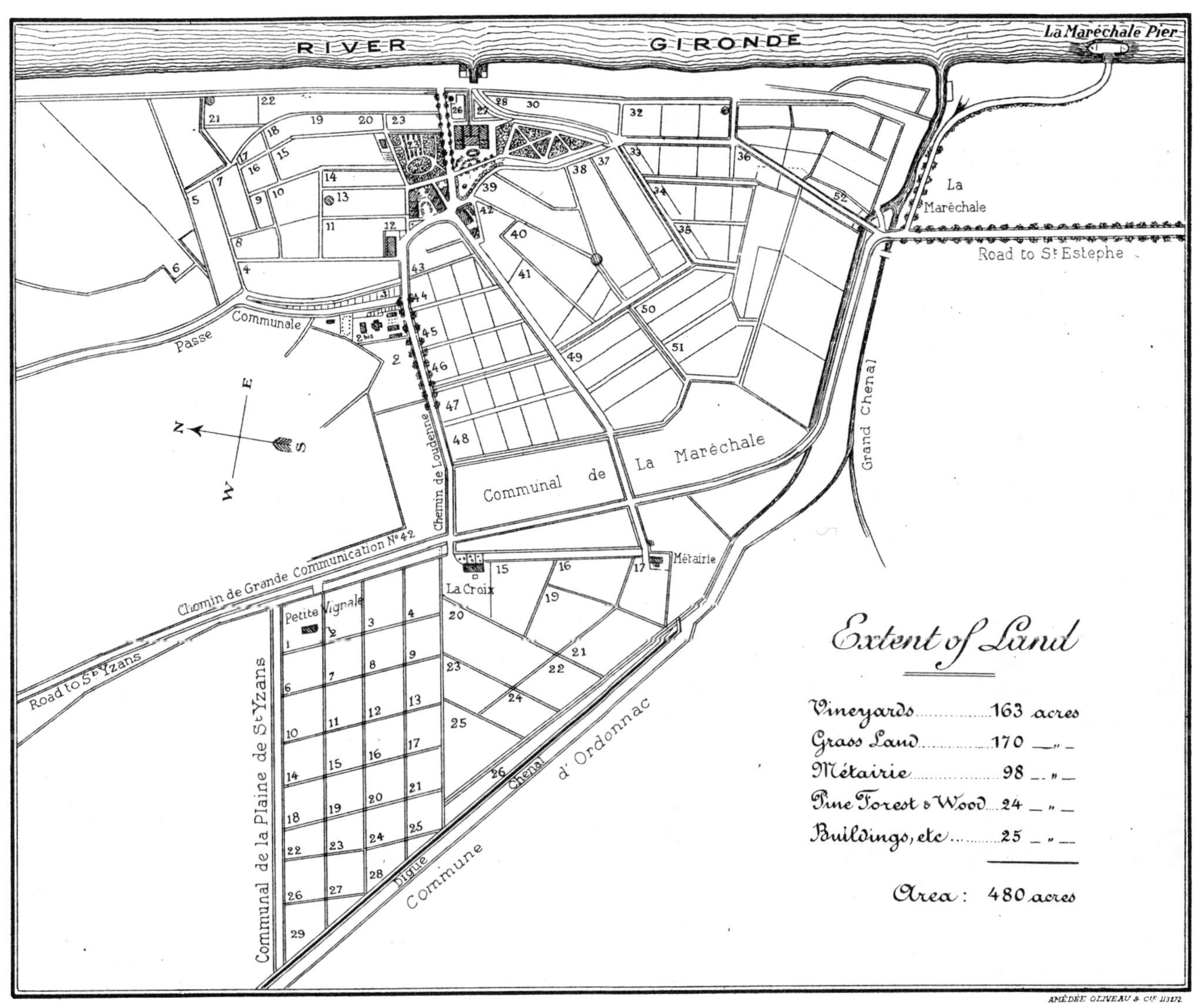

back as anyone can remember each small plot in the Médoc, as in most of rural France, has had its own name, with which it was endowed for some specific reason: for the qualities of the soil, because of some feature or building, because of its proximity to the château or church, or because of some long-forgotten local incident.

The Gilbeys would have none of this: from the moment they bought the estate the fields were to be identified by numbers, not the names by which they are still known on other estates. Even so, the Gilbeys cheated a bit. Ninety years after the purchase of Loudenne, they introduced an excellent brand of Bordeaux which they bottled on the estate, and called La Tour Pavillon*, after the little tower built by Walter Gilbey near the château on a piece historically called La Pavillon, which they had called simply number 13 — just as 'Verthamon', named after the former owners, became number 52 and one M Gabanus, commemorated by a meadow ('Le Barrail de Gabanus') was reduced to a simple number 2. This took a bit of getting used to. In his letters during 1875-76 Brown talks about Le Pavillon 'indicated on the plan by number 13 and number 35 called Le Palan' — and the use of both name and number persisted for some time.

At first it was Brown who was trying to hasten the replanting. He knew that the choicest wines were grown in apparently unpromising gravelly slopes, and the first piece on which his eyes lit was a suitably stoney 2¾-acre field. Only after the vintage visit of 1876, after the chais had been more or less completed, did the Gilbeys turn their attention to the question of vines. Once started they were in their usual hurry: 'We must again express our anxiety', they wrote to Brown in October 1876, 'to get as large an extent of land planted with vines with the least delay.' Their motto seems to have been, 'if it's uncultivated, plant it with vines'. So they ignored the usual rules, and in their zeal planted as near to the river as possible, right down into the inland palus between the château and the road, around the wood behind the new chais and down along towards the little canal and the port of La Maréchale. Within 15 years vines were growing (more or less happily) on 232 acres, nearly four times the acreage they had inherited, and leaving less than 40 acres between the river and the road for everything else: château, garden, woods and ordinary arable crops. And, at first, they were not too discriminating about the varieties they planted.

The results soon showed through. In early 1877 they noted that 'the additional vineland behind the château and by the wood was considered a great improvement'. And the next year: 'A magnificent piece of vineland had been completed and planted, below the wood, along the river and represents an important addition to the extent of vinelands. We were more pleased to see this as it confirms what we had hoped, viz, the probability of, in the course of a few years, getting much of the land at present, to a great extent unproductive, put under vine cultivation.' Within five years they had spent £1,200 on new plantations.

La Tour Pavillon, one of two towers built by the Gilbeys stood on Plot 13; its name withstood the numbering system. Its wine had to be renamed La Cour Pavillon after protests from Latour.

*Following protests by Château Latour the wine had to be renamed La Cour Pavillon.

They were soon congratulating themselves on their investment: 'We were much struck', they boasted in 1882, 'with the improved appearance of our vines in comparison with many of those we passed on Sunday in our journey from Bordeaux to Château Loudenne'. By then they had clearly reached the limit of what could be achieved by orthodox Médocain methods. But as natives of East Anglia, they were confident of being able to improve low-lying fen land. In October 1883: 'It is arranged with Mr Brown to send out from England in the month of November two Lincolnshire fen-men, competent to drain heavy clay and boggy land, to properly stone-drain the two fields, numbers 47 and 48 on the map, before planting or making vineyards, on these two hitherto corn-growing fields'. By this time the Gilbeys were back down the hill to the flat inland palus, for numbers 47 and 48 were (and are, since their numbering system is still in use today) on the pasture beside the main drive down from the château.

They were not deterred: 'These men will also exemplify the method of burning earth as it is practised in England which will in our opinion, be suitable for employment on lands, particularly palus lands, where vines are to be planted, and for making paths etc.' A year later the work was done: 'The large pieces at the bottom of the road leading to the château, about 20 acres, had been drained by English workmen at a cost of about £13 8s 6d an acre, and a portion of it planted with American vines. This drainage work appeared to have been well done, but to ensure its usefulness, it will be absolutely necessary that some good system be adopted for keeping the ditches clean and open so that the water gets away from the land'. A good system was clearly found, for in 1887 they wrote: 'The drainage in the Palus is a great success as the land is dry, whilst all the adjoining meadows are so flooded that they look like an immense lake', and, thus encouraged, they ventured right down to the water's edge. By April 1888 'a new piece of vineyard has been made from a portion of the garden, opposite the Château and promises well.'

The Gilbeys were still aggressively planting after a decade in which they, like every other vineyard owner in the Gironde, had been hit by an unprecedented series of pests and disasters. The resilience they displayed was duly rewarded with healthier vines — and an award from the French government.

PHYLLOXERA
THE FIFTEEN YEARS' WAR

The first 15 of the Gilbeys' years at Loudenne were dominated by two major natural epidemics, the phylloxera and the less-famous, but (for a time anyway) more devastating, mildew. Even at the best of times, in the words of W Beatty Kingston, 'every part of the vine — roots, stocks, leaves, buds, blossoms, and fruit — has special attractions for some noxious parasite, or furnishes for the favourite food of some insatiable insect, which battens and breeds upon it until its vitality is completely exhausted. Fungoids, grubs and beetles are far more inveterate and deadly foes to the vineyard proprietor than frost and hail.'

Kingston's book, *Claret, its production and treatment* — as the author's foreword makes clear — was written with the full backing of the Gilbeys, as part of their propaganda to promote claret; the impressively detailed account he provides of dozens of vine-pests was the fruit of their bitter experience.

Almost as soon as they arrived, the vineyards were visited by the altise, the first of a series of intermittent plagues (other problems were more or less endemic). According to Walter Gilbey, 'in shape, but not in colour, the Altise resembles the Lady Bird, though smaller; the eggs are laid on the underside of the leaves, on which the grubs when hatched feed causing destruction during their growth.'

Loudenne suffered another invasion in the early 1890s. In 1892 'millions of destructive insects swarmed over the palus lands . . . more than half the crop has been destroyed by this insect pest combined with the damage done by the frost'. Three years later the insect alone 'destroyed by damage to the buds and leaves at the least 400 hogsheads of wine'. The next year the altise 'were more numerous than ever and have done an immense amount of damage especially to the vines on the lowlands. Every remedy has been tried to annihilate them, with no satisfactory result.' In 1897 'gangs of women' were 'daily engaged collecting these insects which are to be seen in great numbers, but not so numerous as last year'. In the event, the pests disappeared as mysteriously as they had arrived. By 1899 the altise 'had almost totally departed'. However 15 years later, when the insects reappeared, a chemical solution had been found: 'Great success has been achieved in getting rid of the Altise which has been done by spraying the vines with a solution of Soda Arseniate and Lead Acetate.'

The altise was a well-known, recurrent, menace. The phylloxera, the worst plague with which the Gilbeys were confronted, proved an unprecedented problem when it arrived, four years after they had bought the estate. The phylloxera is a tiny, self-reproducing insect which destroyed the roots of virtually every vine in western Europe during the last 30 years of the 19th century. It had arrived in the Gironde in 1869, but crossed the river and gained a bridgehead in the Médoc only 10 years later. 'It was during this year', the Gilbeys recorded, 'that any alarm was first seriously felt in the Médoc concerning the phylloxera although for some time past it had been making serious havoc more particularly in the Charente and the districts of the Midi. Slight traces of the phylloxera were thought to be apparent in some of the vines of Loudenne on the slope looking to La Maréchale, but Mr Brown hopes to be able to combat this by the aid of sulphate of carbon'. The next year the Gilbeys were still hopeful. 'Here and there one hears of "spots" of phylloxera, and, owing to the extreme winter, some of the vines have failed, but it seems probable that many of the present fears would be a great deal diminished by a fine and suitable season between this and the vintage.'

Within two years they had come to terms with the seriousness of the threat. Thanks to the close contact Brown maintained with Théodore Skawinski at Château Laujac, they had understood the two solutions which were to save France's vineyards. In the short-term, sulpho-carbonate of potassium injected regularly near the roots proved an effective, if expensive and temporary cure. The longer-term solution was more drastic — replacement of the whole vineyard with vines grafted onto American root stocks, which were immune to the disease.

To make matters worse, two other troubles surfaced at the same time: the first was the 'anthracnose', which Beatty Kingston described as 'a cryptogamous disease caused by a vegetable parasite having instinctive affinity to the vine stock'. Its ravages could be prevented 'by a preparation of a sulphate of iron or sulphuric acid, dissolved in water, and applied with a brush to all the wood of the plant, in dry weather only, and before the first week of March.' In 1882, the triple threat was completed by the mildew, described by Beatty Kingston as 'even more injurious in the Médoc than the insect plagues'. It alone continued its noxious activities for years after the wine had been made, kept in cask, bottled and sold. For a decade or more, the buyer of even the most respected growth could never be sure that the bottle he opened would not exude a sour — mildewed — odour and taste. Even bottling at the château — a practice which had become increasingly prevalent during the good years of the 1870s — was no guarantee of quality. The 1884 Lafite proved mildewed, even though the Rothschilds had bottled it at the château, and the trauma was such that the family fought shy of château-bottling for 40 years.

The vintage visit in 1882 was a grim one: 'The Anthracnose, Mildew and Phylloxera, especially the former, have done great damage, the first the more so, even it is said, than the phylloxera; the effect is seen in the quantity of grapes (also leaves) dried up and mildewed, from which no wine can possibly be made. We should have returned very discouraged by this visit except for the fact that, on visiting Laujac, we were impressed by the means which had been taken there to meet all these various evils, and the quantity of American vines being planted served to confirm the idea that this method will probably be adopted as a means of renewing and reinstating the Bas-Médoc vineyards.' They were clearly still hoping to fight the plague in the more valuable vineyards of the Haut-Médoc by the new chemical treatment. Sulpho-carbonate had been applied for the first time that April at Loudenne. 'Mr Merman has adopted the same measure at Le Crock', wrote the Gilbeys, 'and is very sanguine as to the result'.

The following May they recorded that 'during April about 350,000 vines have been treated at a cost of 5 centimes each (about £600) with sulpho-carbonate of potassium and it is thought the operation has been successful, a fortnight's fine weather at the particular moment having been specially favourable for the process, a nursery of American vines, about 30,000 plants, had been planted in the vineyards, especially on the piece below the tower looking to St Christoly'.

That autumn they were forced to undertake another major expense. The new treatment depended on injecting up to seven gallons of chemical into the roots of each vine, so the treatment could only be used by the most affluent and conscientious of growers, able to provide massive supplies of water throughout the vineyard. During their visit in October, they telegraphed to the Pantheon to send out the firm's Jack-of-all-trades, William Hucks. Carver describes him almost lyrically as 'distiller, architect, builder and any other useful work that he could do, nothing came amiss to Bill Hucks. He built the warehouses in James Street, for bottle washing and storing, also for the engineering part of the business, of which he was chief, organising a case-making and carpentering section with up-to-date machinery. . . There was one thing he could never get right and that was the cost of the building or any other work. Excellent in the carrying-out but extravagant in the cost. He was a great favourite with all, both directors and staff, and personally was a most cherished friend and companion of mine despite my complaints of his extravagance' — a remarkable tribute from an accountant.

Hucks arrived within 48 hours and was asked to find the best way 'to conduct water over the estate for the purpose of introducing sulpho-carbonate of potassium to the roots of the vines. He suggested placing a fixed engine at the fresh water sluice, near the wood, with pumping power to force 40,000 gallons per 12 hours through pipes to have hydrants at certain fixed points; from these hydrants the water to be conducted by means of portable pipes to be obtained from the company by whom the vines were treated this year through the principal portions of the vineyards.'*

The high cost of fighting the phylloxera was discussed at length at a partners' meeting in December, although normally the affairs of Loudenne were dealt with on the spot by Walter Gilbey, Ben Grinling and James Blyth, who regularly went there twice a year and who reported their decisions to the other partners. But the matter was deemed 'urgent' (by the rules of the partnership, subjects were allotted only half an hour at their weekly meetings unless they were voted 'urgent' when, seemingly, no time limit applied). The question was simple: should they continue to employ an outside contractor to carry out the chemical treatment, or should they do it themselves? After a long argument 'The Guvn'r' secured reluctant agreement to his proposal that the company should be employed for one more year, but that Brown should be encouraged to experiment by leaving selected pieces untreated to see whether the chemical had to be applied annually.

Viticulturally, the next two years saw the nadir in the fortunes of Loudenne — and indeed of every other estate in the Médoc. The expense of treating the phylloxera was too much for most of the peasant growers, and even the best

*Water was always a problem . In 1876 they had asked Minvielle to 'ascertain the best means of obtaining a permanent supply of good water'. They were forever deepening the well near the house, and early on they installed cisterns and a steam-pumping engine. These improvements proved invaluable during the dry summers of 1892 and 1893, but the Gilbeys were still not satisfied. A specialised contractor was employed to dig deeper — at his own risk. Despite his confidence, the attempt was abandoned in 1905, after he had spent £3,300 digging 1500 feet down without finding water. 'Curiously enough', wrote the Gilbeys, 'there is fully as much water from the old level as is required on the property although the supply is no larger than formerly.'

estates were, for the moment, helpless in the face of the all-pervasive mildew. 'In the Bas-Médoc', they noted in September 1884, 'the results of the phylloxera were more apparent than in the Haut-Médoc for there side by side were to be seen properties that had received the same care and attention as those in the Haut-Médoc and were in an equally flourishing state and those where no remedies whatever had been applied until Phylloxera, couloure or mildew had completely desolated the vineyards. In some places maize and other description of corn had already been planted where vines had been rooted up . . . The sad state of affairs in the Bas-Médoc on the properties of the small-holders in comparison with the healthy and productive appearance of the vineyards adjoining large estates like Laujac would afford the strongest argument that could be adduced against the establishment in England of small peasant proprietors, as a means of meeting the present agricultural depression' — the Gilbeys may have been Liberals, but radicals they certainly weren't.

The year had started deceptively well. 'At our visit in May last', they recorded at the vintage visit that year, 'we remarked that the vines showed promise of an abundant yield. Unfortunately at the flowering time, and in June, the weather was very unfavourable, and although the exceptionally fine weather in July did much to repair the damage, again in August the extreme heat caused mildew and coulure which produced 'shanking' and the grapes to fall to the ground. The general cry about four weeks back was for rain, if the vintage of 1884 was to be saved, and in the beginning of September the desired downfall came, and at the date of our arrival (last Sunday) under its influence both fields and vineyards bore a favourable aspect'. But, on 19th September, only a few days later, 'judging by the appearance of the grapes today they certainly do not look favourable to produce claret of a high character. The grapes are irregular in the bunches, not clusterly and regular in size, and uneven in ripeness the result of bad weather at the time of flowering'.

The results were as bad as had been feared. In May 1885 they lamented that 'the 1884s all through the district from St Julien up to and including the Bas-Médoc are said to be defective owing to the great prevalence of mildew last summer. The mildew appears to have taken almost as much importance as the phylloxera which has been brought under by better cultivation and by many by the use of sulpho-carbonate of potassium'. That year they had treated the vines themselves for the first time — the need for regular annual treatment justified the purchase of the pumps and other equipment.

That October they tried to keep up their spirits by comparing their property with its neighbours. 'The Vines of Loudenne this year', they wrote, 'presented a favourable comparison to those to be seen in the drive from St Estèphe Station. The absence of leaves on the vines in St Estèphe, St Julien, and in the Bas-Médoc generally has been occasioned, it is said, by a visitation of Mildew in the month of August, following the excessive heat of July. This disease destroyed the leaves causing shanking and the grapes to fall from the stalks. Last year was the first time Mildew or blight had shown itself in the Médoc at so late a period of the year. It is curious to remark a similar blight in the month of August this year has caused great havoc to the turnip crop, and in many counties completely destroying this root crop . . . At Loudenne, from some cause, perhaps from the close proximity to the river, the mildew had not affected the vines . . . the grapes as they came into the cuvier were clustery, well-formed, ripe and luscious'.

Even so, it was not a good year to celebrate the 10th anniversary of their arrival at Loudenne — a property on which they had spent in all £70,800 and which they had written down to £42,000 (the Gilbeys were very modern-minded about depreciation, for which they made regular and sizeable provision on all their properties). But they were defiant. Early that year the partners unanimously agreed that 'the figures and all connected with Loudenne were considered most satisfactory', and later that year wrote, 'All those who know the property agree that it has undergone a great change for the better. . . . .'

They refused to be downhearted: 'To commemorate the 10th anniversary we have asked Mr Brown to plant near the château some 5000 to 10,000 roses in the autumn.' This was one of the last instructions they were to give Brown, who had enjoyed an amazingly busy and creative 10 years and was now in his mid-70s. In February 1882 they had noted that 'Mr and Mrs Brown were wintering in Bordeaux on account of Mr Brown's health'. On the May visit two years later they were also in Bordeaux and moved there permanently in September 1885. That month Ben Grinling and Jim Blyth came to Loudenne 'in advance of the usual Autumn party to see that proper arrangements had been made for the due administration of the Estate and Chais by those left in charge' — they spent two days going over the estate with Bayle, the homme d'affaires.

Ever since they had taken over, the Gilbeys had been anxious to secure proper management under Brown. One M Daney, a relic of the old regime, was condemned at the very first vintage visit. According to Mr Brown: 'he never shewed himself so useless as at the beginning of the vendanges'. Over the next decade they recruited a team of three: Aberlen to act as estate manager in Brown's place, and under him Jean Bayle, recruited soon after they arrived to be homme d'affaires, and a maître de chai, M Pascaud. During the 1885 vintage, the set-up was formalised: 'Mr Aberlen had evidently made every effort to conciliate both Bayle the homme d'affaires and Pascaud the maître de chai, and there appears a desire on all sides to work amicably together for the benefit of the estate.'

Brown effectively retired that year, but it was not until April 1888 that they said their final farewells. 'During this visit we had to say goodbye to our friends Monsieur and Mme Brown as the former had decided, in consequence of the state of his health, to retire and go to live near his son-in-law at Angoulême. The early and following pages of this book will show the services rendered by Mr Brown to Château Loudenne and we need only add here our cordial appreciation of the same, and our best wishes for him and Madame Brown for years to come.'

The mid-1880s had seen a complete turn-round in the fortune of Loudenne as a wine growing estate. The first triumph came with the conquest of the dreaded mildew. In May 1886 a meeting was held at Château Ducru-Beaucaillou, attended by both Bayle and Aberlen, 'to discuss the means to be adopted for the preservation of the vines in the Médoc against the mildew, which during the past two years had caused considerable damage and loss of production. Today, Sunday, there is an exhibition with the same object at Bordeaux.'

The solution advocated that year was the 'Bouillie Bordelaise', or Bordeaux Mixture. According to Beatty Kingston, it 'has also been utilised as a specific remedy for the potato disease, and is a combination of sulphate of copper and ''fat'' lime in the proportion of three to one and liberally diluted with water . . . the treatment is preventative not curative, and absolutely indispensable'. It quickly proved its worth. In April 1887, they noted that 'All the vines of the Bas-Médoc appear to have suffered considerably last year with the exception of those vineyards where the preventative treatment against mildew was applied to the vines. This is perceptible in comparing many of the vines grown in the Haut-Médoc and Bas-Médoc with those grown at Laujac and Loudenne'. Naturally prices 'were regulated entirely by the fact of whether the estates had escaped the mildew or not'.*

But the cost of regular chemical treatment for phylloxera was still inescapable. They were treating 300,000 vines a year 'with our own machinery and workpeople'. So they were naturally 'anxious to ascertain, whether in future, it will be possible to treat only a portion of the vines and thus reduce an annual heavy outlay'. They also tried substituting 'sulphur of carbon' which was cheaper than sulpho-carbonate. The money saved on chemicals was spent on manure. Until the 1880s it was unthinkable to manure the vines too heavily, lest they produce too many grapes and thus dilute the quality of the wine (vineyard leases carried a routine clause forbidding the manuring of the vineyard more than once every seven years). But the treatments used against phylloxera so damaged the vines that more frequent manuring became routine — and did not, in the event, hurt the quality of the wine. The Gilbeys inevitably had their own ideas about manure, which, as they noted: 'is somewhat difficult to procure in the Bas Médoc, the price paid is 4 francs per cubic metre and it has to be carted in some cases 3 and 4 miles. The quality is also poor manure chiefly made up of poor litter. Enquiries will be made between now and the winter in Bordeaux as to the possibility of obtaining supplies of manure by boat from there to our port direct. Meantime we have written to Odam's manure company to send out by this week's steamer 5 tons bones, and 2 tons soot, and have left special instructions as to making use of the same in the ploughing which will be carried out during the next fortnight. By this means we shall gain some advantage in saving a year in the application, more particularly to some sickly pieces of vine that require immediate attention.'

The combination of heavy manuring, the conquest of the mildew, and the maturity of the new vineyards, caused yields to jump suddenly in the late 1880s. As they put it in 1889: 'The small production of the estate from the years 1875 to 1884 inclusive is easily accounted for. The vines on the estate at the time of purchase in 1875 were few in number and many of these worn out from neglect etc. During the ten years most of these vines were uprooted and replanted, this having to be done in some cases 2 and 3 times over before success was obtained — four or five years

*Exactly the same applied in 1980, when only estates which had applied modern anti-rot treatments made saleable wine.

in fact were lost in this way.' Although the Gilbeys were infuriated because the vagaries of the weather prevented them from forecasting the size of the vintage until it was actually in the fermenting vats, the increasing yields naturally gave them immense satisfaction. In their first five years, the estate yielded an average of under 300 hogsheads. This dropped by 10 per cent during the dreadful mildew-ridden early 1880s. It more than trebled to 700 hogsheads in the latter half of the 1880s, moved to over 800 during the 1890s — helped by two bumper harvest of over 1,200 hogsheads in 1893 and 1900 — and reached a peak average of nearly 1,200 in the first five years of this century.

The sudden increase in production brought problems. For a start, the whole cuvier had to be reorganised. The three large vats were too large for a single day's 'gathering of grapes' and thus 'unsuitable for proper fermentation' — their size was reduced and additional vats installed in one of the chais. Bayle told them that they could no longer rely solely on 'their own people' to bring in the vintage but must copy other estates and bring in outsiders — 'an additional troup of vintagers'. They, in turn had to be housed, so the cattle were removed from the Ferme de La Croix and the buildings vacated, to be used as makeshift dormitories.

By that time virtually the whole vineyard had been replanted with grafted stocks, although far less precipitately than is generally assumed. 1894 was the decisive year because 'the phylloxera, which has reappeared this year, has made great progress everywhere in France, and has shewn itself in parts of the estate of Loudenne'. As a result, 'from the best informed authorities during our visit we are satisfied that all replanting should be with the American stocks, and graft upon them the cabernet sauvignon vines'. Nevertheless, when they planted an experimental plot the following year they alternated grafted and ungrafted vines. It was only in 1901 that Walter Gilbey could refer to the struggle in the past tense. Referring to the chemicals used, and the replanting programme, he remarked how 'at a considerable expense these two remedies were employed to a successful issue'. The Gilbeys took advantage of the upheaval to improve the vineyard, allowing two full metres (6′ 6″) instead of 1·35 metres (4′ 4″) between the rows, and thus reducing the density from 3,500 vines to only just over 1,600 vines an acre. By the end of the 1880s they were planting lots of cabernet sauvignon, the classic grape variety introduced into the Médoc earlier in the century — they even made the nursery a separate 'profit centre', forcing the vineyard to pay commercial prices for the plants it produced.

Their battles against the disasters of the 1880s did not go unnoticed by the French authorities. At the time of the vintage visit in 1887, they already knew the good news of a forthcoming award. The Gilbeys naturally jumped the gun: 'The report, not yet drawn up by the committee, who inspected the property, is to be issued hereafter, in the absence of this document, and not to speak ourselves of the merit of such an honour, we briefly record a telegram which George Merman of Bordeaux is going to send to The Times and other London Papers:

Viticulture in France: The French government grant annually in each department a Gold Medal for the best cultivated, and the most successful vineyard of the year, and it cannot but interest the scientific agriculturalist to learn that the firm of Messrs W & A Gilbey to improve the growth and character of the vine and arrest the progress of the phylloxera in the district of the Médoc have been so successful as to secure for them the award of the Gold Medal for the Department of the Gironde, a department which includes the most celebrated claret producing vineyards of the world, such as Château Margaux, Lafite, Latour, Mouton Rothschild etc.'

Thanks partly to Walter's genius for publicity, the Gold Medal is the best-known tribute paid by the French to the Gilbeys, followed as it was by the award for the model of the estate at the Paris Exhibition two years later. But a professionally more satisfying recognition came that same year when they received a gold statuette, the 'Objet d'Art', for the grafted vines they had planted in 1886 and grafted a year later and which were already producing a 'good show of grapes' in 1888. A year later they went on a triumphal tour of the estate with their friend M Lalande and his son-in-law, the famous broker M Lawton. 'The waggonette from here conveyed us by the river side passing the port to view the merlot wines between the Gironde and the wood, which vines are particularly luxuriant this year. Driving thence up the old avenue, and as far as the tower on the hill (La Maréchale side) we examined a very successful piece of cabernet sauvignon vines which had been subjected to the

CHATEAU LOUDENNE, MEDOC

"The Lancet" who have carefully analysed Château Loudenne, 1896 Vintage state in their issue of May 2nd that it is an excellent type of Claret, and practically free from sugar and acidity.

The French Government awarded W & A Gilbey in 1900 the highest honour for the superior quality of this Vintage.

Château Loudenne 1896 Vintage is sold in every town & village at 3/- per bottle by W & A Gilbey's 3000 Agents.

Walter Gilbey's 'genius for publicity' ensured that the award of the Gold Medal by the French Government did not go unnoticed by the wine-buying public.

''Provius'' principle — by forcing the more vigorous branches into the earth in order to take root — and scarcely a single plant had missed'. They then had a look at another improvement, the new drive to the château from the south — they had bought the necessary land from one of the Verthamon family the previous year. They were building a bridge, altering the cottage to a proper lodge, and were satisfied that the total cost, including the bridge and alterations to the cottage would be only £400.

They finished their tour by viewing the high vines Malbec, which were the feature of the year. 'Each vine bore a mass of well-formed fruit. M Lalande with his friend expressed themselves as highly gratified and enlightened with their visit and prognosticated a fine future for the vineyards of Loudenne'.

Only a few owners had the Gilbeys' expertise and capital. For the others the combination of increased costs and reduced prices was proving a crippling burden. The Gilbeys themselves drew the obvious lesson two years later, after a visit to Château Laujac. 'While the greater part of the vineyards between Loudenne and Laujac are reduced to a wilderness, the beautiful estate of Mr A Cruze is in a most flourishing condition'. On the same drive 11 years later, 'it was pitiable to witness the deplorable condition of the vineyards of the small proprietors. The like had not been seen since the disastrous period commencing 1884 and lasting some 6 years. The small owners, in most cases, had neglected using remedies against phylloxera, Mildew etc.'

Inevitably the price of estates fell dramatically. In 1886 they noted that 'only a few years ago Mazails, consisting of about 113 acres was, in consequence of the death of the owner valued by the notary at 380,000 francs. Mr Brion of St Yzans advised us in the year 1878 that the real value was about 200,000. Recently the price asked was francs 185,000 and it is quite possible that at the present time it could be bought below francs 50,000'.

Even so, the Gilbeys still poured money into the estate. Early in 1890 Ben Grinling paid a special visit, armed with the partners' authority to build a new chai to house the older wines by filling in the hollow square between the wings of the chais facing the river. Minvielle wanted a classic, part excavated chai, about five foot deep. Aberlen agreed except that he wanted a concrete rather than a tiled roof. But William Hucks wanted a truly modern construction, excavated much deeper and with iron girders. All three were rejected, and in the end Hucks was again sent for, and told to build over the whole courtyard behind the existing chais. Minvielle refused to have anything to do with the work because he didn't trust the concrete Hucks proposed to use. So in the end arrangements were made for 'sending all cement, columns, girders and iron-work from England or Belgium . . . a foreman was to be sent from England to superintend the work'. By this means Grinling hoped to get accommodation for over 4,500 hogsheads in a chai which 'having a concrete roof of seven inches in thickness, should constitute a store of good temperature for old wines, while as it will cover over the existing courtyard in front of the cuvier, it will no doubt reduce the temperature of the adjoining chais . . . The building should take about three months to complete, and when finished it is hoped it will prove the most serviceable store in Bordeaux, or the Médoc.'

Their timetable was absurdly ambitious, but by the time of the regular May visit 'the work had made great progress' and Hucks' only worry was that the contractor would not employ enough men while laying the concrete floor, 'it being of the greatest importance this portion of the work should go on almost continuously in order to obviate the unequal expansion and contraction which would otherwise take place'. Even Hucks was nervous of the new techniques, and stated 'that should the heat of the sun be so great as to cause the cement roof to fracture, it would not destroy its strength as a floor, which can at any time have an ordinary roof placed over it'. But the new design has stood the test of time. The concrete slabs forming the ceiling of the chais still support the mass of material stored on the first floor below the tiled roof.

The cooper's workshop, still in unchanging use a century later, with the cooper refashioning an old cask.

THE BUSINESS OF LOUDENNE

The Gilbeys used Loudenne for its original purpose — as a warehouse and a collecting point for claret — for only a generation after they bought the estate. As soon as the chais had been built, they started shipping wine to England at a rate of 4,500 hogsheads — equivalent to over two million bottles of wine — a year. It was unfortunate that the market peaked just as they were investing so heavily in the estate, in the new chais, and in the vineyard.

Imports of wine from France reached over six million gallons a year in the latter half of the 1870s and then declined to under four million gallons by the outbreak of World War I. Judging by the figures for wines shipped from Loudenne, the Gilbeys' own sales of claret had declined by around a fifth by the turn of the century — although they still disposed of 750,000 bottles a year.

The biggest percentage fall was in the sale of fine clarets for drinking after dinner. Fashion, doctors' advice, the spread of the smoking habit through polite society — and the dreadful quality of the mildewed clarets of the 1880s — all affected sales. As the Gilbeys noted in 1897, when lesser wines were enjoying a recovery, 'the higher classed growths have not been so much affected in value as the consumption in England has fallen off considerably for after-dinner Claret, and the quantity in the hands of the Bordeaux houses is immense'.

The Gilbeys fought doughtily against the trend. For a start they gambled on a grand scale. Even the backing of their unequalled network of agents could not have helped them if their judgment had been faulty, but it rarely was. In 1870 they had bought 1,225 pipes of port (enough to fill nearly a million bottles) after the death of a leading merchant, the Baron de Seixo. These 'light port wines', as the Gilbeys advertised them, 'were bought . . . exclusively for their intrinsic merits' — how dare anyone suggest they were simply picking up a bargain lot — 'and form one of the many purchases which W & A Gilbey are from time to time making to represent their established brands.'

They thoroughly enjoyed a good deal. When Alfred Gilbey and James Blyth visited Jerez in 1874, a 'cut-throat looking gentleman' offered them two parcels of 'dulca' — a wine then much used for sweetening sherry. He was asking only 200-210 pesos for wine which was costing their friend Manolo Gonzalez 350 pesos a butt. Despite the saving they were relentless: 'Finding that the broker was an anxious seller various offers were made and after a telegram to his principal they were closed for at 160 pesos . . . If they are worth a penny', wrote Alfred triumphantly, 'they are worth £10 per butt for buying — these forty butts ought to pay the whole of our travelling expenses for this journey.'

They even turned the onset of phylloxera to their advantage. 'In 1879 and 1881', wrote their official historian, 'when the ravages of phylloxera among the vines of cognac threatened to bring the production of the famous wine-brandy of that district permanently to an end, and did, in fact, arrest it entirely for many years, Messrs Gilbey secured from the stocks of the principal growers brandies to the value of nearly a million sterling.' The purchases were well written up in the press, and the Gilbeys generously shared their good fortune with their customers: 'We are in a position at the present time', they wrote in June 1880, 'to offer to consumers such value in our Cognac Brandies as cannot fail to be appreciated, while in point of quality the undermentioned brands are, we do not hesitate to say, unapproachable at their respective prices.'

When operating from Loudenne, they enjoyed the same advantage over the 'Chartronnais' (the traditional wine merchants based on the Quai de Chartrons in Bordeaux) as they did over the Chartronnais' equally traditional friends and importers in Britain. For the Gilbeys had built up an integrated operation unprecedented in the history of Bordeaux. Indeed, it remained unique until major international brewery and drinks groups invaded Bordeaux on a large scale in the 1960s. But they were not, strangely enough, competing with the Chartronnais for the ordinary wines they required for their basic clarets A, B, C and D. (In an attempt to boost sales, the previously somewhat stark labels were changed in the mid-1880s and the four provided with descriptions: A was simple Bordeaux, which came mostly from the palus and from Blaye across the Gironde, B was Bas-Médoc, C Médoc, and D Haut-Médoc, descriptions which still correspond to today's claret hierarchy). But the Gilbeys' English clientèle demanded a much lighter type of wine than the heavier clarets (previously fortified with stronger wine from elsewhere in France) demanded by the traditional claret buyers. 'The Bordeaux houses always welcome a vintage wine with deep colour and full body', they commented on the 1895 vintage, 'as such clarets are valuable for giving to a thin vintage what is needed'. In the same way the 'excessive heat' of the summer of 1892 'is thought by many to be against a wine appreciable by British consumers. It will have color and body resembling the 1865s and 1870s and wines of this type are always saleable by the Bordeaux Houses. It is the quality of the '64s, '75s and '88s that are wanted for the English consumers'. These required a mixture, preferably from two consecutive vintages with diametrically opposed qualities. 'The 1893s', they — more probably James Blyth — wrote in 1896, 'resemble the 1865s in possessing great body themselves, and being immediately followed by a year in which the wines are very right and exceedingly cheap. The blends of 1865 and 1866 produced most charming, soft, medium-bodied "vins ordinaires" which were greatly appreciated in the Exhibition year of 1868, and did much to stimulate the consumption of light wines in England'.

The French themselves wanted even tougher wines than traditional British drinkers. 'The wines of the 1890 vintage', they wrote, 'will have immense color and which is certain to cause a demand for the cheaper descriptions, for consumption in France where red wines are consumed at all meals, much diluted with water.'

Like their rivals, the Gilbeys were faced with rising supply and falling demand throughout their first quarter century at the château. In 1878 they reported: 'The large vintages of 1874 and 1875 and the increased vineland that has come into bearing the past few years have placed the production of medium and fine wines far ahead of the consumption and the result has been that many of the proprietors in the Haut-Médoc have had three vintages in hand' — generally they preferred to sell as much as possible immediately after the vintage. 'Coupling this with the general depression of commerce throughout Europe it is not surprising to hear that most of the wealthy merchants of Bordeaux are "choke-full" of wines.'

This pattern soon repeated itself. In September 1884, they found that 'the depressed state, throughout the world, of trade generally and the consequent complete stagnation of the Bordeaux market had compelled the proprietors to submit prices that had not been known for very many years' — so the Gilbeys leapt in and bought. In 1893 'the opportunity to secure matured wine, ready to bottle, of really good quality, has not occurred since the abundant vintages of 1874 and 1875'. The reasons were the same in both cases: 'The cause of prices ruling so low is that the Bordeaux houses being full of stock and upon many estates the wines of the last two and three vintages remain in the hands of the growers.'

It was crucial to pick the right vintage. They were not invariably successful in their choice. They had great hopes of the 1883s: 'With their good color and their soft flavour, coupled with the very moderate prices at which they can be sold in England, we contemplate as great a success in their introduction as attended the 1875s or even the 1864s.'* So they bought half Château Latour's production, a quarter of Lafite's, a third of Léoville Lascases' and Grand Puy Lascoste's, and the whole production of Montrose, Mouton d'Armailhacq (now Mouton-Baronne Philippe) and Lynch Bages, as well as 'many others'. But, like virtually all the wines of 'the mildew years', they were not a success. By the late 1880s the Gilbeys were clearly in a hurry to get rid of them. 'The clarets of this vintage are undoubtedly wines possessing considerable elegance while their lightness of character renders them fit for early consumption. They may be said to represent a type of wine especially suited to the English consumer's taste during the summer season. All these wines have been bottled in France, either at the château where produced or at Château Loudenne.' The prices were tempting, with Haut Brion and Latour available at 48s a dozen.

But none of the vintages of the 1880s lived up to the 1875s. The Gilbeys had been early and major buyers of this magical vintage (including the whole production of at least two classified growths, Rauzan-Sègla and Langoa Barton). It proved to be a wine-merchant's dream. By 1880, 'although only five years old and two and three years in bottle, most of these wines have now arrived at a stage of perfection when they can be consumed by connoisseurs with satisfaction. The greater proportion of these will, however, continue to improve for many years to come and will certainly take rank next to the famous 1864s'. Unfortunately even these fine wines were difficult to sell. Even before the onset of the mildew 'the general depression of trade coupled with the growing taste in England for beverage wines is calculated to keep down the price of the classified growths'. So in June 1880 they produced a 'Special List' of 'High Class vintage clarets of the year 1875', and a mouth-watering selection they were too. The biggest quantities on offer naturally came from their two 'exclusivities' — 67,255 bottles of the second growth Rauzan Sègla at 48s a dozen, and 78,773 bottles of the third growth Château Langoa Barton at 42s, both 'bottled in the Médoc', almost certainly at Loudenne. But the thousands

*Then, as now, it was part of the game to compare vintages. Before they bought Loudenne 'poor Henry Southard' had called the — clearly heavily-sugared — 1869s 'Sweetmeats'. And they made the comparison at least twice, with the 1878s and the 1890s which they found 'particularly soft and sweet'.

CHATEAU LAFITE

BOTTLED AT THE CHATEAU

1875 VINTAGE

W. & A. Gilbey

CHATEAU MARGAUX

BOTTLED AT THE CHATEAU

1875 VINTAGE

W. & A. Gilbey

VIN ORDINAIRE

Bottled by W. & A. Gilbey

CLARET

CHÂTEAU LOUDENNE

VINTAGE 1881

of even grander bottles on sale — from Lafite, Margaux, Mouton-Rothschild, Léoville Barton and Cos D'Estournel — were all 'bottled at the Château' in the spring or early summer of 1878, two and a half years after they had first fermented. Bottom of the list came their own wine, Château Loudenne, at 24s a dozen (although they were soon offering an '1875 Vintage claret. The produce of the Médoc district, purchased from the estate, direct from the grower' at a mere 21s a dozen).

The 1875s continued to enchant, almost to mesmerise, the Gilbeys for the next 30 years. In that miserable year 1884, they were cheered to find that the 1875s 'never shewed to greater advantage that at present, particularly the Langoa and Château Margaux'. Even so, the pressure to sell them remained intense and in 1886 the partners authorised James Blyth to sell another 3,000 dozen of the Rauzan-Sègla. By 1893 the price had doubled to 8s a bottle (with Lafite at 11s and Margaux at 12s 6d). But the price-list stressed how the wines 'were purchased soon after the vintage and the prices quoted are lower than on the wholesale lists of the Bordeaux shippers'.

By 1890 the wines were worshipped as the 'now celebrated 1875s', but by 1898 the few remnants still in stock were all showing signs of decline. Even in 1912, when they tasted several bottles of old claret with two leading Bordeaux merchants, they found that the 'Léoville Lascases and Château Margaux 1875 were well preserved'.*

*There is some discrepancy between the Gilbeys' ideas and those of subsequent generations of connoisseurs. Although both sides would agree on the quality of the 1875 vintage, the Gilbeys were looking for wines that matured much earlier than some of the vintages — like 1870 and 1893 — so greatly appreciated in the inter war years. These were simply too tannic and slow to mature for the commercially-minded Gilbeys.

If the 1883s proved disappointing, most of the other vintages of the decade were simply disastrous: 'The best that may be expected of the 1885s', they wrote in May the following year, 'is that they may turn out like the 1881s which with plenty of colour begin already to show signs of harshness and dryness, and are really only suitable for imparting color to their unfortunate thin and weak successors the 1882s.' No wonder they welcomed the vintage of 1887. It 'will be most valuable, not only to consume by itself, but to give richness and color to those wines of the past vintages which need those qualities'.

They had even higher hopes of the 1888s. Initially these were so promising that the Gilbeys paid a special visit to Loudenne in March 1889 to taste them: 'We came to the conclusion that the quality resembles very closely the famous '75s', they reported excitedly. The Gilbeys managed to buy a considerable share in dozens of leading growths, including Margaux, Lafite, Mouton Rothschild, Rauzan-Sègla, Langoa, Palmer, Pontet Canet — and even Pape Clément from the Graves, not an area from which they normally bought much wine. The trade agreed, and had bought heavily: 'many of these have since changed hands at a profit'.

In May 1890, the 1888s retained their appeal. They had 'all the delicacy and elegance (softness) so much appreciated and in demand, and being very forward are exceedingly useful, and the more so seeing the lack of such quality in preceeding vintages, at the same time their moderate price is also an important element'. Later that year they had 'every confidence 1888s will rank high and become hereafter celebrated'. They needed such a success. In May

1891 they hoped that 'in five or six years from now — when the faulty wines of the years 1882-3-4-5-6 shall have disappeared from the cellars of the wine merchants — such good vintages as 1888 and 1890 will be the means of resuscitating the claret trade of England'. It was not to be. In April 1898 the 1888s appeared 'somewhat thinner but have developed no additional flavour'.

As early as 1893 they were being offered at knock-down prices, with even Lafite available at 5s a bottle. They had to wait until 1900 for a vintage fit to rank in their estimation with their beloved 1875s. That year they remembered 'how much the appearance of the grapes resembles those of that year; and the want of moisture which was needed for the overripe grapes of that year (1875) is equally noticeable this year'.

By then the buyers had the upper hand. The whole trade recognised that the 1899s had been 'exceptionally good' and 'trade in the higher qualities was in a more animated state than it had been for years . . . but all this has now (May 1900) subsided owing partly, no doubt, to the splendid promise for an abundant crop of grapes this year . . . there are still large parcels of the unclassified growths of 1899s in the hands of the growers. Such wines would be of great value for shipment to England, but in the face of the fine vintage prospects of the coming vintage it is thought advisable not to add to the already large stocks in the Loudenne Stores, as it is quite possible these prices may decrease'.

They were right. In 1903 they wrote bluntly: 'The 1900s have one great advantage over the 1899s as coming second in two successive years, the prices at which they can be bought are less by 33 per cent. Under these circumstances they can be purchased of the Bordeaux merchants to sell at lower prices than high class clarets have reached the public for many years.'

By 1903 it was clear that both years were remarkable, and there were great arguments over their respective merits: 'The 1899s have today undoubtedly more flavour and colour. On the other hand the 1900s have a remarkable softness and delicacy, which coupled with sufficient colour, make them most fascinating wines.'

Because the Gilbeys were owners as well as buyers, they were ambivalent about the slump. If the 1900 vintage was selling badly, it had also effectively destroyed the value of the excellent 1898 vintage — of which the Gilbeys themselves had been major buyers. 'Château Montrose was sold this week at £7 per hogshead against £22 paid last year for second growths'. Lesser growers were even worse off. Château La France, 'which ranks as a first growth of Fronsac, situated on the banks of the river Dordogne, sold at a price equal to £2 5s a hogshead. In reckoning the cask as worth this year 15/- this will leave but 30/- for 48 gallons of wine, which is less than 9d per gallon.' Elsewhere things were even worse: 'In the Saumur district 500 hogsheads of red wine from one estate sold at 12/- per hogshead without the cask.'

For all their disappointments they did at least manage to establish their own château's wine on their wine list. Their dream — like that of hundreds of other proprietors since 1855 — was to see its qualities duly recognised by promotion to the cherished status of 'cru classé'. 'Doubtless, when the classification of 1855 shall come to be

125

Visit – Vintage 1900.

Land at Naujac. – The woodland at Naujac being in dispute as to a few acres, instructions were given Mr Samuel Hucks to write Mr Bonniol, notary at Lesparre to see into the matter and settle the dispute. – See page 118 –

Exchange of land at Loudenne. – Since the visit in May, piece No 1 of Loudenne land has been exchanged for a piece of the same size belonging to Mr Bonnet A – The land referred to adjoins the Farm Buildings or to the field adjoining –

Up-rooting Low-land vines. – Instructions given to continue on up-rooting unproductive vines – see pages 57 and 59 – A plan showing the pieces agreed to (and signed) has been added to the minutes. –

Replanting. – Several pieces of old vines were condemned and consent given to replant this year. These pieces are also shown on plan in the minute book. –

Land to be planted with vines. – It was decided to replant the piece of land, No 52, about an acre at the entrance, near the Lodge.

Hay Crop. – The hay crop was got up in splendid condition, and the quantity, 170 loads is above an average. – For the yearly production from 1890 to 1899 – see page 115. –

Cattle. – In June 8 young steers were purchased to turn out upon the rough lowlands, where vines had been uprooted – They are now on the meadows, across the St Yzans road and are growing well, in excellent condition – Those bought in June 1898 did well and nearly doubled themselves in value in 12 months. –

reconsidered', wrote W Beatty Kingston in 1892, 'certain of these "bourgeois" or rather "château" wines such as Laujac, Loudenne, Le Crock, Bessan, Sigognac and Verdignan will obtain the honours of classification.' (The list was carefully chosen: apart from Loudenne, Le Crock belonged to the Gilbeys' friend and broker George Merman, Laujac was run by their mentor, Théodore Skawinski, and they had always liked Bessan since they nearly bought it in 1875.)

But this ambition was never fulfilled, and until the 1960s Loudenne occupied an undeservedly humble place in an increasingly rigid hierarchy. The pinnacle of snobbery was probably reached by the Irish barrister, Maurice Healy. In the late 1930s he wrote in *Stay me with Flagons,* 'speaking of good, cheap wines, I should like to say a word of praise of Château Loudenne, an estate owned by Messrs W & A Gilbey and lovingly fostered by them . . . it may gratify Messrs Gilbey to know that when I shared my mother's house, no matter what I offered my guests or drank myself, there was always a bottle of Château Loudenne for her own consumption, and I did not despise a glass of it myself' — thus reducing the wine to the level of that other successful Gilbey product, invalid port.

For all the Gilbeys' aspirations, Loudenne's status as a 'bourgeois' growth fitted the requirements of their clients. But most of their attention (increasingly so as the market turned away from fine wines) was focussed on the cheaper wines. Their purchases were irregular, if sizeable, and the biggest single influence on their size and timing, as on the quality of Loudenne's own wine, was the weather.

The numerous comments on the weather in the Loudenne diaries bear all the hallmarks of Walter's passionate, almost obsessive interest in the subject. Occasionally the conditions were extreme enough to fascinate even the most blasé observer. A September gale in 1895 had one curious effect. 'On the windward side of the trees, hedges and vines the foliage was turned to a deep brown as if burnt whilst on the sheltered side it remained as green as in July. A similar gale took place four years ago and the same effect was noticed. The cause of the change of color may be accounted for by the salt spray from the sea carried inland by the strong westerly gale (equinoctial)'. And like every other vineyard proprietor the Gilbeys were sometimes the victims of freak conditions. In 1880 the crop was reduced by two-thirds by a hail storm. It was 'purely local, affecting principally Loudenne, Senilhac and parts of St Seurin, in reality it lasted only 4½ minutes when hail stones fell in size almost as large as pigeons eggs and apart from destroying about one fourth of the vintage at Loudenne it also did considerable damage to the tiles on several of the buildings.' But Walter Gilbey went further. Readers of his letter to *The Times* after the 1891 vintage, for instance, were treated to a long discussion of whether the previous three decades had shown a return to a new ice age. He even used the recently republished records of weather in 14th-century Lincolnshire kept by a contemporary parson: 'Evidently the farmers and vine growers of 1343 were no more free from weather anxieties than their descendants of 1891', Walter assured readers of *The Times,* 'and yet there is a crumb of comfort for the latter in the fact that both corn and the vine still flourish.'

Like many other Englishmen before and since, Walter

Gilbey assumed that Bordeaux was simply an extension of southern England, and that therefore its climate should be roughly the same. He was forever comparing the temperature with its equivalent at his Essex home at Elsenham and was affronted when it differed. At the time of the 1892 vintage, 'it is strange', he wrote from Loudenne, 'with such fine weather here that each day's news brought the reverse from England, "rain", "cold", "occasional frost at night".' And the pessimism of the previous year had quite disappeared under the influence of a wondrously hot summer: 'In passing through Paris' he noted that 'all the trees on the boulevards presented a burnt and rusty appearance. The like high temperature had never been recorded in the 160 years of observations of the meteorological Society of France.' The weather at Loudenne was equally without precedent in the memory of the firm's partners — which now extended a quarter of a century back to their first visit in 1863. 'The thermometer in the library* recorded never less than 69 and was frequently 71. This room facing the north never has the sun upon it. As each year since 1887 has been improving, it is to be hoped a cycle of favourable seasons has set in, in comparison to the many summers previous to that date.'

He was right. The weather the next year remains without parallel in the Médoc. 'After a very temperate winter, the weather up to the beginning of the month of May was all that could be as desired . . . the flowering set in earlier than had been the case in any year since 1865 . . . the summer was extremely dry . . . the heat was almost tropical during the weeks preceding the commencement of the vintage'. On 17th August, indeed, the thermometer recorded 112° Fahrenheit. The vintage started four days later — over a month earlier than the average date (September 27th) on which it had begun since the Gilbeys bought Loudenne.

During the vintage 'there were two days of rain doing an immense amount of good'. It 'did wonders in causing the grapes to swell and give them all that was needed to perfect the wine . . . it will be strange if the 1893s do not rank amongst the best quality clarets of the century.'* But a year like 1893 was a freak in a region where the quality of the wine can never be taken for granted. Uncertainty about the weather — and thus the size and quality of the vintage — obviously affected prices. In 1879 they seemed 'ridiculously high . . . should the prospects of the next vintage not improve, all the wines here will probably be cleared off by the end of June'. The weather throughout the growing season had been terrible, the worst since 1816 when, in Champagne at least, 'the grapes were not thought good enough to gather and allowed to rot on the vines'. In 1879 the vintage started on October 11th, later than at any time during the Gilbeys' first 20 years at Loudenne. And it was

*The small reading-and-writing room just off the main salon

*Their enthusiasm soon cooled. 'It is most fortunate that we were not purchasers of the classified growths of 1893', they wrote in 1896, 'as notwithstanding the favourable comments of the English press, our original opinion is daily being confirmed that they possess too much body ever to become elegant clarets like the 1864s and 1875s', although this did not stop them advertising the 1893 Loudenne as possessing 'good body and elegance'. They much preferred the Sauternes, and bought 375 hogsheads in the Spring of 1894. 'It is many years since such fine white wines were made in the Bordeaux white wine district', they wrote later that year, 'and as a consequence those remaining in the hands of the growers have advanced 50% in price'. By 1896 their 'magnificent stock . . . could not be replaced at double what they cost'.

only at the very end that they dared begin to hope: 'In examining the grapes both on the vines and as they come into the cuvier on the bullock wagons they are full size well coloured and sweet, increasing each day in size and sweetness by the sun and dew — most people would say such combined qualities will make good wine . . . since writing the above . . . dull cold days with frost at nights have set in, the grapes coming to the cuvier are observed to be much smaller, thicker skinned, and less juicy, particularly those from the cabernet sauvignon vines grown north of the château'. In the end the wines turned out generally poor and thin.

A late spring frost could — indeed still can — completely upset the market by reducing expectations for the forthcoming vintage. In 1876 'the prices will depend very much on whether there is a frost or not during the coming spring'. And in 1892 they were congratulating themselves on the wines of the three previous vintages they had 'bought under favourable circumstances on the day preceding the severe frost of April 19th'.

If the prospect for the vintage was good, then the merchants would buy 'sur souches' before the grapes had even been picked. In 1880 'many of the Bordeaux houses were tempted to do what they had never done before, viz to make purchases in advance at high prices of the 1880s wines not yet made'. But then the weather turned rotten and the purchases stopped. (It was only in 1898 that the Gilbeys were tempted to buy before the vintage for the first time. They ascribed their boldness to the favourable reports obtained from Paul Aubert, who had spent a week in the St Emilion district — where the vintage is often earlier than in the Médoc.)

The merchants themselves also set the purchasing pattern. In October 1879 'large quantities of 1878s have been sold in consequence of the speculation set on foot by Mr Lalande.' And in November 1891 the Gilbeys set the pace. They thought the Langoa Barton and the Pontet Canet the best of the year: 'Bearing in mind the popularity of the latter brand we determined to negotiate, which ended in our becoming the purchasers of two thirds the growth, viz, 600 hogsheads at 850 francs per tonneau. This transaction virtually opening the campaign of the '91s, many sales taking place in quick succession, so that half the classified growths were purchased in a week.'

But the death the previous year of their broker, their 'old and much esteemed friend Monsieur Eugène Baguenard', combined with the decline in claret sales, gradually took the zest from the gambling game. They mourned Baguenard: 'he had indeed made himself one of us . . . his death . . . cannot but fail to be regarded as a calamity to all interested in the wine trade'. Although they came to trust a number of other brokers, who were always welcome visitors at Loudenne, by the turn of the century they no longer had the need for the sort of regular attendance which Baguenard had provided at Loudenne. By then buying the wine had become something of a hobby, without the commercial importance it had enjoyed back in 1875 — and the same could be said of the estate itself.

THE OLD ORDER CHANGETH

In retrospect, the purchase of Loudenne can be seen as marking the peak of the Gilbeys' fortunes. Although the firm continued to prosper after 1875, Loudenne's purchase was the last of the bold strokes that had astounded the world of wine in the two previous decades.

The Gilbeys had come to dominate the scene. In return, they, who had been outsiders attacking an establishment grown smug and sleepy, themselves became the target of attack for newcomers. Nor could they, in a receding market, expect their share to grow — in fact sales reached a peak of 850,000 dozen in 1876 and only regained that level in the 1890s. Although they sold over a million cases a year for a few years at the turn of the century, the trade was much more concentrated at Christmas time (by 1900, the single month of December accounted for nearly one fifth of their total annual sales). Moreover, margins had been cut to the bone. They were being undercut — at least one chain of off-licences, the Victoria Wine Company, was advertising claret at 10½d a bottle, and they themselves had to reduce the price of their sherry to a mere 1s. As Carver grumbled: 'This craze for cheapness had a serious effect on profits, as people naturally went for wine at such a low price, especially as they were really good wines for the money. Unfortunately the sale of better class wines declined.'

The Gilbeys also suffered from the Model T syndrome, the classic disease afflicting a firm which has enjoyed quick and exhilarating success through following one particular commercial formula: they found it impossible to change. So it was with off-licences, the major chink in the Gilbey commercial chain. They may have been buying direct from the grower, but they were not selling directly to the consumer. But their one investment in a pioneering chain of off-licences proved a disaster. Carver tells the story with an accountant's bleakness:

> 'Leverett and Frye were Grocers and Wine and Spirit Merchants, etc etc. The managing director was F C Frye, a relative of the Crosbies (the maiden name of Mrs Alfred Gilbey).
>
> W & A Gilbey financed this business by advancing money for opening fresh shops in districts where we wanted a good agent.
>
> The business was started in 1872 and money was advanced which amounted to £57150 by 1889.
>
> In 1894 it was turned into a Company with Preference Shares £27,000 and Debentures £30,000 issued to W & A Gilbey as security.
>
> F C Frye was elected MP for North Kensington and was supported by the Off Licence Association as representative of the Trade in Parliament.
>
> The management of such a large number of shops, together with the duties of the House of Commons proved too much for him and Mr Argo Gold and myself carried out an investigation of accounts which proved to be very faulty. It was decided to sell the business to the International Tea Stores retaining only the Irish business. A large sum had to be written off as lost, the accountants had not properly ascertained the financial position each year.'

The shock was such that the Gilbeys did not again venture into the field until the 1930s, when they made a more successful investment in Foster & Co.

More serious was the problem of brands. The Gilbeys' great strength had been the relentless exclusivity they gave to their 'Castle' name. This may have been synonymous with purity and good value, as the Gilbeys claimed, but it lacked class. Predictably, they first encountered the problem over that symbol of luxury, champagne. In 1880 they were forced to remove the labels from their own brands of champagne. They explained to their agents: 'As sparkling wines are not decanted like Port and Sherry, but must of necessity be placed on the table in the original bottle, we have been induced to make the above-mentioned change, and we do this the more readily as we are well aware that, when judged simply on their merits, the wide difference in price will be recognised by the more discerning Public between certain of our standard brands of Champagne and precisely the same wine which we know are now being offered by various shippers under many well-known French names, at from 15/- to 20/- per dozen higher, although, strange to say, being what are called proprietary articles, they are amongst the most unremunerative part of the English Wine merchant's business.'

Alas for the Gilbeys they were helpless in the face of the 'proprietary' articles. But they fought hard: the first breach of the 'Castle' walls in 1882 was restricted to Champagne.* It was only eight years later that they finally gave way. The precedent was set by John Jameson, the favourite brand of Irish whiskey — which, until the 1880s and 1890s sold much better than Scotch. They had close links with 'J J', and the brand benefited greatly when they put their formidable commercial machine at its disposal.

By then the situation was grim: 'It is hoped', says one partner's memorandum, 'that our travellers have exaggerated when they tell us that a third, or at least a quarter, of our agents are breaking conditions and buying Brandies elsewhere'. So they were in a weak position to negotiate with Hennessey and Martell, recognising that they would have to sell their brandies 'with scarcely any profit to ourselves rather than see our agents dissatisfied and inclined to break conditions'.* They also had to add other familiar names — Gonzalez Byass' sherries, Ingham Whittaker's marsalas, Burgoyne's Australian wines, and Croft's ports — to their lists.

In their heart of hearts, they never abandoned their dream of selling only their own brands. When Jasper Grinling first joined the firm in the early 1950s, he found that in one corner of their vast Camden warehouses, 'workers were solemnly decanting Croft's Vintage Port into fresh bottles labelled with the Gilbey brand of 'Cantos' — even though this would cut sharply the price at which the wine could be sold. But Croft had been a wholly-owned subsidiary since 1910 so the Gilbeys could sell it how they wished.'

Even worse, the Gilbeys totally misjudged the mass conversion of so much of the drinking public to blended Scotch whisky in the last quarter of the 19th century. Their

*The Gilbeys still tried to load the odds against the dreaded 'Proprietary brands'. Prices of their own champagnes ranged from 24s 6d to 68s a dozen; the cheapest 'proprietary brand' came from their friend Mr Ayala and cost 64s a dozen. The most expensive brand was Pommery & Greno at 103s — even Bollinger, the fashionable favourite of Edward VII as Prince of Wales, was 'only' 90s.

*A complete contrast to the balance of power 18 years earlier. In 1874, when Alfred Gilbey was arguing with Ingham Whittaker, he had emphasised the importance of the firm's purchasing power 'by drawing a sad picture to him of how Martell had declined our overtures when first made to him and then repented after it was too late.'

blindness does credit to the clan's pride in the purity of the products they sold. In the early 1880s, Charley Gold, the partner in charge of their Scottish business, 'was shown how the profit on whisky might be considerably increased by adding patent, still grain spirit', in the words of the firm's official history. 'But no advantage was taken of this information by the firm, because they were of the opinion that genuine whisky could not be produced except from malted barley, and that customers asking for whisky were entitled to receive spirit distilled from that and no other grain'. They did distill their own malt whisky, but it was not until 1905 that they were prepared to sell their own blended whisky. Until a few years earlier they had still been prepared to testify in court that only spirit made purely from malt was entitled to the name whisky. In 1902, they had even launched 'Spey Royal' in commemoration of the Coronation of Edward VII, emphasising that it was pure malt. (The next year that indefatigable publicist, Walter Gilbey, now a septuagenarian baronet, compiled a booklet 'showing the advantage of Pot Still Whisky'.)

By then, unfortunately, the firm was in no state to face these challenges. The death of Alfred in 1879 had removed the mainspring for commercial initiative, and only the unquestioned authority of 'The Guvn'r' kept the naturally disputatious partners together. As one obituary of Walter Gilbey puts it: 'Henry Parry Gilbey . . . calm in judgement and temper, who, as long as he lived, was regarded by the firm as its counsellor, whose judgement was the final court of appeal on matters of policy, and whose sweet and tactful disposition was a great power in reconciling differences, interests and personalities in a gigantic firm'.

His death early in 1893 was a disaster. He left nearly half a million pounds, and the Gilbeys have always claimed that it was the death duties levied on the estate which led to the transformation of the partnership into a limited company. Its size revealed the true extent of the business for the first time. The company's tangible assets amounted to £1,280,000 and the share capital was £1,440,000 — a difference which allowed something for the firm's enormous goodwill. But there is another explanation for the change. The first articles of the firm provided that the shares could be held only by a director or by a direct male descendant of the original holder. 'The Guvn'r' had two sons, one of whom, Charley, had died in his teens; the other, Percy, survived until 1919 but is never mentioned in the family's archives. It may be that the company was formed because the other partners wanted to buy out the shares left by 'The Guvn'r' and also enable his daughters to receive their due. After all, death duties, in their modern form, were introduced only in 1894, a year after he died. (The will created endless problems: Henry de Rivière, the Cognac broker who had married Henry Parry's elder daughter Laura, contested the will and Carver had to go to court to prove the figures were correct.)

Even more severe problems were caused by the allocation of the original share capital in proportion to the informal share of the profits previously paid to individual partners. Walter's allotment was far and away the biggest, largely because he had been one of the original partners. This did not suit James Blyth at all. With some justification, he felt that he had contributed at least as much to the firm's profits as Walter, and he went to the lengths of hiring a

QC to dispute the allocation. He was never a very amiable character ('he is hated where he is best known', was the crisp summing up of one Liberal election agent some years later), but his key role as wine buyer, and his indefatigable travels, had earned him parity with Walter. Nevertheless Walter won, and James Blyth withdrew from active management, although he continued to visit Loudenne regularly until 1914 and supervised the buying.

In all this upheaval Loudenne was bound to suffer financial pressure. In 1890 Walter Gilbey was firmly — and correctly — predicting that the estate's production of wine would leap in the future as a result of the heavy outlay of the past decade. This increase would, he said, 'give consolation to those members of the firm of W & A Gilbey who seldom visit Château Loudenne'. He was clearly referring to Charley Gold, who came for the first and last time in 1880 — and who presumably resented the capital being lavished on Loudenne because he needed the money to build up the firm's Scotch distilleries (by comparison the three surviving members of the 'Loudenne four' visited the estate between 35 and 39 times apiece between 1875, and 1891 and Henry Arthur Blyth came 14 times. Apart from Charley Gold, only his brother (six visits) and 'The Guvn'r' (five) fell into the category of infrequent visitors.)

The doubters and the opponents obviously increased their pressure when 'The Guvn'r' died, and a special sub-committee of the Board was appointed to deal with Loudenne's affairs. It included two of the original four, Walter Gilbey and James Blyth, Alfred's elder son 'Allie', one of his younger brothers Newman, and Ben Grinling's son, Gibbons Grinling. The committee reflected the family balance and also reinforced the trend that in each generation there was a small group of 'Loudennites' ready to defend the estate against all attacks. The minutes of their first meeting in September 1893 reveal that the estate had made an overall operating loss of nearly £8,000 since they had bought it — although it had been profitable for four of the six years since the mildew was first conquered in 1886. So they drew up two sets of accounts, 'one showing the working of the property as a Wine-growing estate, and the other as an entrepot for storing wines' — allowing the estate £1,000 annual rent for the chais.

By the beginning of 1895 it had become glaringly obvious that the problem lay with the wine-growing side, whose losses more than absorbed the profits made by the chais — although the profit accruing to Loudenne as a business has always been somewhat notional, since it depends on the price paid by the parent company for the wines purchased and stored at Loudenne. The sub-committee was faced with a loss for 1894 of £2,860 before allowing for £1,000 annual depreciation of the estate's value. This was mainly due to the disastrous 1894 vintage — on top of the greatly increased costs of cultivation during the disease-ridden 1880s. The result was a mood of grim reality: 'The committee are more than ever convinced as to the difficulty of making a profit on our French estate.' The key cost was the £7,000 spent on cultivating the vines. The solution was obvious; to restrict production to the best acreage on the estate. Already, in 1893, their friend Paul Aubert had been asked to work with Aberlen and Bayle in trying to deal with some of the most low-lying pieces of land.

By the end of the decade, nearly 100 acres of vines, 40 per cent of the total, had either been uprooted, or were under sentence of death, being pruned 'à mort' in the winter and deprived of nourishment in the summer. Of course no ordinary viticulturalist would have planted vines on the low-lying pastures on which the Gilbeys imposed them; once these pastures had been ploughed up, the vineyard, concentrated on the gravelly slopes round the château, proved capable of making wine of infinitely better quality.

But the diehards were not going to give in without a fight. Walter Gilbey, a fanatical 'trencherman', was still convinced that if only the land were properly trenched, then vines would grow well anywhere. 'It is greatly to be deplored', he wrote in April 1894, 'that those who advised us, including Bayle, should have been mistaken in planting vines on low-lying heavy land, without first trenching the ground. It was generally believed by us that in preparing the above-named pieces of ground (about 50 acres) for vineyards, the land was to be hand-trenched, and it was only after our last visit here, we discovered to the contrary.' Even the best bits of the vineyard had not been properly drained, which made it easier for Walter Gilbey, supported by Bayle, who naturally wanted as large an acreage under vines as possible, to blame their problems, encountered everywhere, onto bad drainage. Bayle was ordered to drain one piece (number 43, by the archway entrance), 'the cost of which in England would not exceed £3 per acre'. But 'to do the 2½ acres would cost £50 if done by our usual French contractor. Sir W G will send three men from England costing for conveyance by steamer including wages for £15 and they will execute the work in three weeks.'

But the committee was on the defensive. Early in 1896 it emphasised 'the strenuous efforts made by the Loudenne Committee to reduce the Expenses as much as possible'. And even Walter could not hold out against the damning evidence that the 67½ worst acres of vineyard had produced a mere hogshead an acre — a fifth of the yield from the better plots.* The Committee promised a 'definite decision . . . in the meantime, as instructed by the Board, no more money than is absolutely necessary will be expended on the pieces referred to'.

Walter Gilbey still refused to admit that they would have to uproot the low-lying vines. The 'special men sent from England' the previous year had duly decided 'that the bad appearance of vines in various places on the hills was attributable to land being water-logged'. Later that year he remarked that 'except the low-lying vineyards which have been improperly planted, and the young plants which were allowed to get water-logged from bad management, the vineyards on the whole looked remarkably healthy and well'. It was also clear, to Walter if to no-one else, that the fault lay solely with inadequate digging. 'It is also evident', he wrote, 'that the low-lying lands have not been dug sufficiently deep. The roots on numerous pieces showed that their stunted growth was attributable to the hardness of the sub-soil.' He would only agree to uproot 16 acres, 'the remaining pieces to continue under vines at any rate for a few years, to see the result of the Altise'.

The reprieve was only temporary. In January 1897 the

*Even this rate represented over 30 hectolitres of wine per hectare, three-quarters of the yield permitted for such vineyards under present French legislation.

sub-committee 'proposed to adhere to the arrangement made in January 1896 for the reduction of the vineyards to 140 acres after the vintage of 1897' — and, as earnest of its intentions, cut the budget by £1,000. At the May visit, Walter Gilbey accepted defeat, although he found his own explanation for it. 'The prospect in the future of buying good cheap wines in the Médoc, coupled with the knowledge gained in working this heavy land', was the reason for uprooting so many vines. 'In reading these notes it may be thought strange that such an outlay should have been incurred in making vineyards on such low-lying heavy soil, but when it was decided to plant vines on these pieces, the wines of Bas-Médoc were fetching from £6 to £8 per hogshead, whilst today good wines can be purchased from both the Haut- and Bas-Médoc at from £3 to £4/10/0.' (Even then, Bayle fought a rearguard action over 44 acres, which he believed would produce a proper yield once free of the Altise.)

By May 1899, the Committee could report that the cost of the vineyards had been reduced by £1,200 a year in the four years 1895 – 98, compared with the first four years of the 1890s. As a result, although the losses were not entirely eliminated, they were contained to a few hundred pounds. Nevertheless, in 1903 the Loudenne Committee had to write down the value of of the estate by £1,000 a year to a mere £25,000 — less than the purchase price a quarter of a century earlier.

Walter Gilbey was also defeated over the animals required to work the estate. In 1894, he was admitting that 'in the future it was thought advisable to purchase large Normandy horses for ploughing instead of the shire horses brought from England, and Mr Aubert was instructed to ascertain the price of suitable animals' (though he still would not admit the suitability of the French animals. As he wrote four years later — after one of the regular parades of the horses and oxen on his estate — 'there is no doubt the English horses are not only the best, but are the cheapest').

It was left to Newman Gilbey, on behalf of the Loudenne Committee, to downgrade these noble animals. In 1906 — when the estate's requirements for draught animals had obviously diminished because of the reduced acreage under vines — he wrote that 'one great reason for importing the heavy cart horses from England was to cultivate the palus which was too great a task for the oxen. It ought not to be necessary to replace these horses, but to do all the farming with oxen.' Nevertheless, tradition had been established. And in 1911 when George Bayle, son of the first 'homme d'affaires' asked for 'six good horses for the haymaking season' he expressed a preference for the horses to be sent from England. The number of oxen was increased, not only for use as draught animals, but also because bullocks could be fattened on the excellent and well-drained pasture formerly planted with vines.

Loudenne only became a truly model and agriculturally well-balanced estate in the 1890s. During the decade, the chais were extended and improved and the estate's own wine vastly improved . . . once the vines had been confined to the slopes around the château. At the same time more attention was paid to the varieties of vines planted on each piece. 'It was decided some time ago', Walter Gilbey noted during the vintage visit in 1899, 'to plant some more

Malbec and Merlot vines; it has been done on several pieces, and is now thought advisable to continue planting them as the proportion of Cabernet Sauvignon vines is much greater in acreage than the Malbec and Merlot. The principal object is to produce at Loudenne an improved quality of wine.'

The Bayles, father and son, (who ran the vineyard itself continuously from 1875 until World War II) were clearly in favour of the merlot — the early-maturing variety also much favoured in St Emilion and Pomerol, against the cabernet sauvignon, which provides the backbone for most the Médoc's better wines, but which matures later and thus creates special problems for vineyards like Loudenne in the northern half of the Médoc (the vintage can be a week later at Loudenne than in Margaux, 25 miles to the south). Indeed, until the 1960s, the estate had a far greater proportion of merlot than is usual in the Médoc — a fact which did not prevent the 1961s, for instance, from being classic, long-lasting wines. The preference was a natural one, for Loudenne's heavy, clayey, soil suits the merlot very well.

The specialisation of the vineyard was carried further in 1899, when — at Bayle's suggestion — they planted a few thousand grafted semillon blanc vines to produce white Bordeaux. Test planting were made on a number of plots. This followed an earlier experiment in making white wine in 1893 (and a private purchase of white grapes in 1898 by Walter Gilbey). The new attempt worked. Within five years they were making 20 hogsheads of white Loudenne and production has been continuous since then, although the quality has varied widely. Overall, the estate was clearly making more wine than was required, and they even toyed with the idea of making sparkling Loudenne — from 'a pressing of red grapes Cabernet will be made and kept separately*.

They had already started sending some of their surplus production to Saumur. At vintage time 1892 they had sent 'four hogsheads of Château Loudenne to our friends Messrs Ayala to make into sparkling wine. Unfortunately the wine was damaged by sulphuring the casks before shipment. During this visit (vintage 1893), two hogsheads of Château Loudenne 1893 were sent to Messrs Ayala and two to Ackerman Laurence to make into sparkling wine.'' The experiment was so successful that by 1902 they were sending 100 hogsheads a year to Saumur.

(In those days, makers of sparkling wines adopted a pretty cavalier attitude to the geographical origins of the grapes they used. In 1874, Alfred Gilbey recorded how the price of champagne had been effectively halved within a few months: 'This was brought about to a great extent by the Champagne merchants having procured wines from other White Wine districts of France, such as Burgundy, Sauterne, etc, etc.' Nevertheless, the sparkling wines of Saumur remained cheaper, and the Gilbeys had introduced them the following year with their usual flourish, referring to the wine as the favourite of the 'modern French humourist Balzac', and emphasising especially the 'hygenic qualities necessary to recommend it to the sick, the infirm and the convalescent'. In their wine book, the Gilbeys had

*They had also economised on the wine they provided for the workers. Because of shortage of wine in the bad years of phylloxera, they had bought 100 hogsheads of 'the cheapest suitable wine to give them. It is decided to return to the old custom and make this year ''vin de sucre''. In making ''vin du sucre'' the skins from pressing 100 hogsheads of wine, from the grapes, will materially assist in making a wine suitable for the workmen.'

mentioned how champagne, 'owing to its rapid action as a stimulant and restorative has obtained a high position in the opinion of the profession, and in cases of great prostration or exhaustion it is highly valued, as its action is more immediate and harmless than that of brandy'. The introduction of the cheaper imitation, they told their agents bluntly, would be 'a means of extending our Agents' connection among a class of consumers who attach great importance to Medical opinion').

The remodelling of the estate was a major preoccupation throughout the 1890s. One result of the chill wind of economy was the further reduction of the garden, which originally must have stretched down to the river. In the late 1880s, the acreage of lawn had been reduced and replaced by a new piece of vine-land, Number 23. But the layout was still formal, with a central flower bed and a circular path round it, according to the contemporary plans of the estate, and it was too much for one man — 'one gardener not being equal to keep up properly so much vegetable land and paths'. So a further acre of lawn was to be planted with various varieties of grapes — including some for table wine — as an experimental plot (they were still hoping that it would be possible to replant the vineyard without resorting to grafted stocks all the time). Even then they kept their rose bed, the group of figs to the left of the lawn, and the elms, the apples and the Osago orange tree in the lawn itself, and planted vines only to the right of the lawn nearest the chais; they also ordered 6,000 roses, at a cost of £20, to form a hedge from the lodge at La Maréchale up to the wood. The tendency to use the garden, and the labour-intensive vegetable garden in particular, as a sacrificial gesture in the times of financial stringency, has remained a recurrent feature of the management of the estate.

In defiance of the prevailing mood of economy, they also systematically replanted the woodland and avenues on the estate. When they took over, Madame de Marcellus told Edouard Brown that the wood had not been cut back for nearly half a century; 'the small avenue from the terrace leading to the river was the result of allowing the trees in

The park avenue leading down to the Gironde. 'The appearance of the estate today remains the result of the efforts made in the 1890s.'

two ancient hedgerows to grow'. Apart from bringing a young aloe 'from a rock at the lighthouse of San Sebastien near Palafrugell', they did very little until the early 1890s, when they started to clear out the old and dying trees. 'The land', wrote Walter Gilbey in 1895, 'to be trenched and replanted with different varieties such as birch, elm, oak, fir and ash'. They found not a single tree 'in the entire wood growing upon his own roots, they are the remnant of a coppice which used to be cut down at intervals, consesequently the present trees are growing upon the old stubs very much decayed'. Not all their efforts were successful. In particular the 70 plane trees planted on both sides of the drive from La Maréchale all died and had to be replaced by locally grown tamarisks and acacias from the wood.

They eventually replaced virtually every tree on the estate — importing over 1,000 willows from a nursery in Saumur. Apart from the elms — recent victims of the dreaded Dutch elm disease — the trees have largely survived, and the appearance of the estate today remains the result of the efforts made in the 1890s.

So it was appropriate that the last real honour paid to the estate was in 1901, when the Agricultural Society of the Médoc awarded Loudenne its Gold Medal and Diploma for the best cultivated vineyard. At the award ceremony that September, the Mayor of St Yzans struck a practical note: 'Our parish, as though touched by a fairy's wand, benefited by their presence as our neighbours. The people have found work, and several proprietors, both large and small, have had the opportunity of disposing of their wines to British commerce . . . they have done much good by the example they have set in the management of their vineyards.'

In reply Sir Walter Gilbey was decidedly more flowery, providing a potted history of the firm's efforts since they purchased the estate, referring, rather tactlessly, to the Gold Medal of 1887 as 'the greatest honour my firm ever received'. He finished by 'acknowledging the honour the Society has paid to two of our staff, namely Mr Samuel Hucks, our Estate manager, in presenting him with a silver salver and diploma to our bailiff, Mr Bayle, a silver medal for long service.'

One name was conspicuously absent from the award ceremony. It was that of their former estate manager, Mr Aberlen, who had been sacked five years previously — his only consolation, £70, six months' salary, 'as recognition of his past services'. The reasons for his dismissal are not given in the archives, but the parting was clearly brusque. He left early in May 1896, leaving behind debts of 2,000 francs to the butcher and the baker. 'We thought it advisable', wrote Newman Gilbey, 'to square these by paying half'. The only consolation was that 'two of Aberlen's sons are working at Loudenne and giving satisfaction'.

Over the previous years, Paul Aubert had worked with Bayle in transforming the vineyard, but the Gilbeys entrusted the management of the estate as a whole to Samuel Hucks, son of the trusty William. He was paid £120 — soon increased to £150, 'and it was further proposed to retain the services of Jean Bayle, who has now been with us for over 20 years as "homme d'affaires",' and as such, was responsible for the vineyard. Working with him was his son George, and about this time another family of Loudenne 'trusties' emerges with the name of a certain M

Gombeau, the maître de chai, and his young son, Camille. The family were local wine-growers, mentioned as peasant proprietors in early editions of Cocks and Feret's viticultural bible.

The Gilbeys were still taking a close personal interest in the running of the estate. The Loudenne ledger for 1900 has survived and goes into the tiniest detail — from the annual wage bill (something over 4,500 fancs) down to vet's fees of 250 francs, fly paper for 10 francs, 44 francs 70 centimes spent on 'rope for the flagstaff', and a bill of 4 francs 20 centimes for one of the Médoc's first telephones. Yet at the same time they were, effectively, writing off the property. The original impetus for its purchase had gone. Loudenne's place in the Gilbey galaxy had dimmed with the decline in the claret trade, and the original partners were growing old. In 1900 the Loudenne Committee admitted defeat. The members naturally regretted the continuing losses, although they expressed themselves satisfied with their efforts at reducing them so sharply in the previous few years. They admitted that, on average, the wine from the estate could bring in only an average of £6,200 to provide for expenses which were bound to exceed that amount, yet 'the estate has a certain annual value to the company as an advertisement, and for the facilities it affords for the collection, treatment and shipment of Clarets and Sauternes . . . as a set off against the amount written off the property may be placed the amount which Loudenne is valued as an advertising medium.'

The Loudenne sub-committee seems to have been disbanded in 1900, but the Gilbeys handed over responsibility for the estate to the locals only in 1906. The withdrawal became the occasion for a small-scale battle between the two families, the Gombeaus and the Bayles. They were both obviously telling the partners that they could run the estate on only a light rein from London — a position usual in the Médoc, where absentee owners have often left the running of their estates to generations of 'régisseurs'.

The arrangements were complicated by the death of Jean Bayle early in 1906. This reinforced the Gombeaus' position, and they won the key battle that all George Bayle's activities would be recorded — and thus to a certain extent supervised — through the office, the Gombeaus' domaine. This was an unusual arrangement: since the 'homme d'affaires' ran the vineyard and paid the workers, he was normally entrusted with supervising an estate's finances. So George Bayle had good reason to feel aggrieved. James Blyth, who was supervising the transfer of responsibility, was firm: 'we do not want to interfere in any way with the purchases made by George Bayle . . . but we hold the strongest opinion that everything connected with cash and the bookkeeping must be concentrated in the office, so that at all times we may know what amount has been spent in the various departments, as well as the money which has been paid out for goods' — in the absence of their masters, local régisseurs habitually took a percentage from local suppliers.

The division of the spheres was spelt out clearly. Although George Bayle was not to take over all his father's work, yet he was to be entirely responsible for the vineyard, for the farm and its buildings. The chais, the garden, the woodland and the office were to be the Gombeaus' domaine — and although they were to be responsible for the château, both families were to have keys to it, symbolising their equality. But it was Camille Gombeau who was clearly the favourite. He is described as 'a smart young fellow' by one of the partners, and was the recipient of much warmer letters from James Blyth than were sent to more ordinary employees. More crucially he was given power of attorney over the estate. Nevertheless, the battle between him and George Bayle continued, the latter refusing to admit Gombeau's supremacy until he died in his 70s during World War II. He had lived at Loudenne since he was six, for his father had been engaged as 'homme d'affaires' a mere nine months after the Gilbeys had bought the estate.

Two years before the handover, Sir Walter Gilbey had retired from Loudenne and relinquished the supervision of the estate to Sir James Blyth. That same year came a revolution in transport which was to transform Loudenne socially from a modest venue for working family holidays to the scene of those ostentatious house parties so beloved of the Edwardian rich. In September 1904, notes the diary, four of the party arrived from Bordeaux by motor car. The availability of cars cut down the journey time. By 1909 Blyth and three Gilbeys 'proceeded to Loudenne' from Bordeaux by motor car and managed the trip from London in 20 hours — rather faster than the same trip could be accomplished today without going by air.

The arrival of the motor car emphasised the contrast between the rule of Sir Walter and the reign of Sir James. By 1904 they were, allegedly, barely on speaking terms — it is even said that they used different drives to the château — and even if that was a family legend, the visitors' book shows that 'Sir Walter's party' was quite distinct from 'Sir James and his friends'. While Sir Walter was generally accompanied by local friends of no great distinction, Sir James had an obvious taste for the high life*', and was already famous for the dinner parties in London where he entertained the future Edward VII.

They were already improving the accommodation in the château itself: they bought two more 'cast-iron baths' — complete with bath thermometers and other fittings: they lashed out on carpets, a barometer, a 'hot water apparatus', and a set of drawing room curtains to replace those chosen by Mrs Brown a quarter of a century earlier. In 1903 they arranged for 'a small cellar in the caves at Loudenne, as at Lafite and Mouton, where we shall retain a few bottles of each well-secured growths of the Médoc. We shall then have all the years of Loudenne to compare, also the choice growths of the Médoc'. This type of 'vinotèque' is quite a normal fixture in the major estates, and its belated introduction at Loudenne shows the relatively spartan nature of the Gilbey's previous accommodation.

The motor car reinforced the change to a more social régime. Previously Loudenne had been so isolated that any visits to estates in the southern part of the Médoc involved a major effort. By 1905 — when 'Mr Henry Cruse and his son called in his motor car on his way to Château Laujac' — such visits had become easier and encouraged greater socialising, which itself transformed the nature of the visits. The Gilbeys tended to hire cars for the duration of their

*And for the ladies. According to a story Camille Gombeau told his successor, Charles Bouilleau, Paul Aubert's wife (' a truly beautiful woman') was Blyth's mistress for many years at Loudenne.

'Before World War I, the visitors' book became very largely the record of a series of "house parties" ', with 'the strong atmosphere of an English country house'.

stay. Other visitors tried to motor from as far away as Marienbad, although they often broke down en route, and the adaptation to the horseless carriage was not complete. In one entry, Lord Blyth refers to a trip with two cars 'with Gombeau on the box' of one of them; and in a letter to Gombeau discussing the proposed purchase of a car, Lord Blyth says, 'if we could hear that the man who looks after the pump understood driving an automobile it would no doubt increase the prospect of our having one instead of a horse*'.

Nor was the transformation entirely smooth. In 1909, Gordon Gilbey's drive from Bordeaux 'took an hour longer than usual on account of repairs which were being done to the road nearly all the way'. And just before the war, they mention 'an anxious drive home' from Langoa Barton, 15 miles away, 'as the Chauffeur had not brought lamps' — a laconic understatement for anyone who knows just how dangerous the winding Médocain roads still are at night, even for drivers equipped with 'lamps'.

In the nine years before World War I, the visitors' book becomes very largely the record of a series of 'house parties' — itself a term not used in the book until 1907. Blyth's guests were a mixture of Liberal politicians and of aristocrats (the Earl and Countess of Jersey, Viscount and Viscountess Mersey, Lord and Lady Bellew, Viscount Selby and the famous actor Sir Squire Bancroft) providing the strong atmosphere of an English country house. They even played that most Edwardian of card games, bridge.

To the locals, the château had clearly become 'the big house'. There is only one record of protest and that goes back to the early 1880s, when a Spaniard called Pascal was seen by Mrs Brown wandering around the house. When arrested he said bitterly, 'there they were playing billiards and I haven't got a penny in my pocket'. But respect was generally the order of the day. Carver remembered going to the Catholic church at St Yzans, where they 'were ushered to special reserved seats with "Prie-dieus" (kneelers), and the congregation remained standing until we had taken our seats, and when the service was over, no one left the church until Monsieur et Madame had passed down the centre aisle to their carriage! We felt ourselves some "Pots" '. Although by that time a number of members of the family had been converted to Catholicism through marriage to daughters of their Spanish friends, the respect shown to the Anglican Carvers was purely social.

Not that the Gilbeys were generous squires. In 1904 they allotted a mere 500 francs to local charities. The Curé received 200, the Bordeaux sailors' reading room a mere 100, the same as the sum allocated to the 'Culte Reforme' in the Médoc. More obviously worthy causes, like the sisters looking after the old or abandoned children, received only nominal sums. But the Curé himself was a regular visitor to the château. 'The Curé and Mayor of St Yzans came to déjeuner', records one note, 'and had a very heated discussion on the separation law' — the bitterly disputed proposal to separate Church and State. The reference to déjeuner sets the tone, as do repeated references to 'café au lait'. By then, social life was formal: Carver — one of the

*The same lordliness towards new forms of transport lasted until the 1960s, when a director proposed that the firm buy an aeroplane. The driver of the Gilbey coach and four, could, it was said, be retrained as a pilot. Since the said coachman was elderly and notoriously alcoholic, the suggestion was turned down.

few employees to visit the château after the turn of the century — remembered how on one visit 'the large Central Hall was filled with a table whereon was a display of fruit and flowers, and the usual cutlery and glass necessary. The dinner was a means of tasting and discussing the merits of various Vintages of the most famous Vineyards. I remember having about six or more glasses, and waiter murmuring in my ear 'Lafite Soixante quinze', the choicest wine of a memorable year, and we had six different vintages to taste.'

The old routines started to go by the board. It was recorded that 'No visit was paid to Loudenne as is usual in May 1906', but the absence of such a visit was not even mentioned in subsequent years. And the traditional Vintagers' Ball had been abandoned; it had to be revived officially in 1911 at the express wish of the staff. 'Mrs George Bayle explained that it was much appreciated not only by all the people on the property, but also by the troupe of vintagers who are specially engaged, the thought of which she assured us, encourages them all to take a greater interest in their work. The Ball, therefore, was held this evening and special musicians were engaged for the occasion. On entering the Vintagers' Ball Room six bouquets of flowers were presented by six small children to the six ladies of the Loudenne Party, all the ladies and gentlemen taking part in the opening dance and a very enjoyable evening followed' — an entry which is worlds away from the regular informal affair described by Somerville and Ross only 15 years earlier. More typical was an afternoon when they 'motored to Langoa to take tea with the Bartons, they being alone. Spent a pleasant couple of hours with them seeing the pressing with the feet (with fiddle) in the old fashioned style.'

By then the continuing decline in the sales of claret, and Lord Blyth's elevated social station, had changed the business apect of the visits. Whereas previously their stay in Paris had been punctuated by visits from their trusted suppliers, by 1906 Sir James Blyth spent the day 'calling by appointment on Sir Henry Austin Lee and the British Ambassador, Sir Francis Bertie on the Wine Duties, and the Anglo French Exhibition' — of which he became Honorary Treasurer.

Buying, if not forgotten, was no longer a major preoccupation. At the vintage visit in 1912, they spent the morning tasting the 1909 and 1911 wines in stock. But 'after déjeuner Lord Blyth with Mr Newman Gilbey and Captain and the Hon Mrs Claude Rome' — the former Grace Loudenne Blyth, who acted as her father's hostess at Loudenne — 'left by motor for Bordeaux and the two former spent a couple of hours in Messrs Barton and Guestier's chais, tasting fine sauternes, and a few of the 1911 clarets. The Hon Millicent Blyth with Miss Lisa and Miss Carmen Gilbey followed in the second motor, and the seven dined in Mr Eschenauer's house'. Where previously they had dealt direct with the growers, now they were working through the Chartronnais; where previously social life — and their women folk — had come a bad second to their work, the two were now intermingled.

At least they mostly were. But the note of the vintage visit ends: 'Mr Gordon Gilbey and the Hon Mrs Gordon Gilbey remained in the château for another week'. Gordon Gilbey was the elder son of Alfred's second son, William

Crosbie, who had married a Spanish lady, Miss Gordon (the accent is on the 'don'). And by 1910, at the age of 24, he had emerged as the dominant connection between the firm and the estate. In 1911, he married the heiress to the ancient Catholic barony of Vaux — one of the few titles which can be passed through the female line — and he was to spend the next 50 years looking after Loudenne and defending its interests against an increasingly vociferous series of attacks.

In the last few years before the outbreak of World War I, however, he was still optimistic about the estate's future. He worked hard — 'tasted in the sample room till dark' goes one note. He reported religiously on the developments in the wine trade, especially the arrival of Algerian wines, 'a topic of daily conversation in Bordeaux', because they were so prolific and so suitable for the French market that they threatened the whole structure of viticulture in the Midi. He continued the family tradition of inquiring more deeply than the locals into the chemistry of the wine they were producing: 'We have never studied the question of acidity (either tartaric or acetic) and from what we have gathered they have never paid the least attention to this question in the Médoc beyond the information obtained from the estate, although for years it has been the practice of viticulturalists, or rather Wine Merchants, in Champagne and Burgundy to do so by analysis . . . we have collected all the information on this subject that we could.' He ensured that the port was properly repaired. He 'had an interesting conversation with Bayle on his father and the early occupation of this property' — maddeningly, he did not elaborate on this unique insight (for 'young' Bayle had been six when his father had arrived as homme d'affaires).

But his closest relationship was with the young Camille Gombeau. In 1910 he 'had several talks with Gombeau with reference to starting this business' trading in wine, especially to the hotel and restaurant business trade, in France itself, from which the Gilbeys themselves were debarred. The estate had been the property of the partnership, and, to avoid stamp duties, had never been included among the assets transferred to the new limited company. It remained, in theory anyway, in the former partners' possession, so they could not use it as a base for conducting their own business. Gordon Gilbey thought Gombeau a 'smart young fellow . . . and I see no reason why, if we arrange a plan for him to start on this business, he should not meet with success'. Gordon Gilbey was even prepared to set up special stocks at Loudenne to back up Gombeau's idea, and by 1913 was 'devoting a great part of his time to the Hotel department of France' — a notable concession to someone supposed to be a full-time employee.

In 1913 Gordon Gilbey seemed happy with the state of the property. The weather, admittedly, was bad. If it did not change 'the quality must be inferior as the grapes are suffering terribly'. But he saw everything else through a rosy mist. 'Bayle and the two Gombeaus get on very well together, although they keep to their several departments, and there were very few suggestions that we could reasonably make to improve the general appearance and diminish the cost of working the property . . . both first class men and suited to their posts, as Gombeau Senior is also, and indeed all the staff male and female . . .'

It was to be his last visit until 1919.

Camille Gombeau, one of the two 'long-lived, obstinate guardians' of Loudenne. His stewardship preserved the château and the estate through two world wars.

THE SLEEPING BEAUTY

With the outbreak of World War I, Loudenne went into a decline which lasted nearly half a century. During the war itself, the estate was cut off from London and kept going largely by Bayle. Gombeau had been called up, and predictably entrusted the power of attorney over the estate to his wife rather than to his rival. But even after 1919 it never regained its old status. This was hardly surprising, for conditions had turned full circle. Sales of claret in Britain remained miniscule, and could be satisfied by small, irregular purchases in the Bordeaux market, usually carried out through the indispensable Camille Gombeau. So the chais, which had been fully occupied until after the turn of the century, remained virtually empty — after World War II they were even used to store wines made by the local cooperative. The château fell into an increasing state of disrepair, and its social attractions died once Lord Blyth stopped coming after 1914. Intermittent — although largely desultory — attempts were made to sell the estate, but the market remained depressed throughout the inter-war years, indeed, right up to the boom of the 1960s. The survival of the estate depended on two long-lived, obstinate guardians, Gombeau, who died in 1957, and Gordon Gilbey, who survived until 1964.

Loudenne was just one of Gordon's responsibilities within the firm, which changed astonishingly little until well after World War II. Until 1945 the shares could only be held by a direct male descendant of one of the original partners: and it became a tradition that only the eldest son of any director entered the firm. The whole system became formalised, almost fossilised, and although the firm survived and even prospered, it was a very different phenomenon from the days of the first generation. Sir Walter had retired before World War I and had died in November 1914. He spent his last 10 years writing, with considerable outside help, an annual volume on different aspects of equine history, and building up his unrivalled collection of sporting paintings*. His arch-rival, Lord Blyth, survived until 1925, but in his last years was chiefly occupied with his obsession, universal penny postage, on which he wrote innumerable letters to *The Times.*

After Sir Walter's retirement, the chairmanship was supposed to rotate every year — an arrangement which implies a good deal of mutual suspicion among the four families. But in 1910 Gordon's father was elected chairman and remained in the chair until he died in 1926. Even Carver, who had little time for most of the founder's offspring, found him 'an ideal chairman . . . He was beloved by all, and we missed his genial personality and buoyant spirits.' He was succeeded by Henry Walter Gilbey, a swashbuckling, moustachioed figure straight from an Edwardian novel, nicknamed 'The Champion' and a favourite of the gossip columns. (In 1935, when he was well into his 70s, he was quoted as saying that he found women 'expensive but worth it'. He had married his first wife back in 1884. After her death he married again, exactly 50 years later, and a year later had another son.)

One of 'The Champion's' favourite occupations was teasing his poor cousin Gordon about Loudenne. Gordon was an ideal butt, and could always be relied on to rise to

*After his death they were promptly sold, at the worst possible time, by his son, Henry Walter, and formed the basis of the Mellon collection. Many other American collectors hurrying over for the sale were drowned on the Lusitania.

the bait. One of the family remembers Gordon emerging quivering and white-faced from a board meeting, followed by the cheery figure of 'The Champion' slapping him on the back and offering him a drink. The symbol of those years, remembered by all concerned, was a cartoon drawn by 'Tony' Grinling, Ben's grandson, showing Gordon as a tortoise with Loudenne on his back, and the distinguished figure of 'The Champion' urging him to get rid of it. But Gordon was stubborn and a hard worker in a generation which preferred to spend the ample funds accumulated by their parents rather than increase the family's inheritance. He was an ideal defender of the beleaguered estate.

Nominally, Gordon was one of the two directors responsible for the curiously named Bonded Stock Department. Until the 1960s, this seems to have been responsible for all the firm's activities — buying, shipping, dealing with overseas subsidiaries — except for the specific functions carried out by the home and export sales departments, and by the financial controller. Gordon's other director was his cousin Sebastian, universally known as 'Bassy', who 'worked hard at playing hard . . . he would breeze into the office, ask Gordon if everything was alright and then breeze out before Gordon could even reply'.

This attitude was typical, and in the interwar years the only initiatives were taken by Arthur Gilbey — Bassy's father — in foreign markets, especially in Australia and Canada, where Gilbey's Gin became a major market force (abroad he was allowed to change the taste, but the partners refused to tamper with the historic, rather flowery formula used at home). But in general the firm coasted along, and sales drifted, progressively more dependent on the Christmas trade. In the mid-1920s, December accounted for over a quarter of the annual total, itself only half the pre-war figure. Gordon himself was too bound up in routine business to have the time to take any initiative: his life was spent in an endless round of work, either at the Pantheon, or on his regular tours of the family's interests in Europe. Of these, the relationship with Gonzalez Byass in Jerez and the Croft business in Oporto were crucial, for with the decline in sales of table wines, and the continuing inability of the family to capture any important share of the market in blended scotch whisky, the sales of sherry and port had assumed even greater importance. Loudenne occupied a minor place even in Gordon Gilbey's scheme of things.

In the 1920s this did not matter, and the estate merely ticked over happily enough. We have two quite separate accounts of life there at the time. There are the relatively dry details conveyed by Gordon Gilbey, Alec Gold and other directors during their regular visits in the first half of the decade, backed by the directors' minutes of the rare occasions when the affairs of the estate were discussed. Then there are family legends. These concern especially Henry Arthur Blyth's grandson Derek (other versions refer to his uncle, the second Lord Blyth). The story goes that one of these was in the habit of taking a large party to Deauville, that his only visit to Loudenne was by special train, and that before he would condescend to visit so outlandish a spot a tennis-court had to be built. The only — indirect — evidence of this legendary trip is that a tennis court was indeed built as early as 1921 directly in front of the chais, a casually arrogant gesture of disdain for the few

During the 1920s 'the estate merely ticked over happily enough' — visits by the family became scarcer, but there were still some local gatherings on the terrace at Loudenne.

'A noticeably restrained celebration of the 50th anniversary of the purchase, when a mere £100 was voted and spent on entertaining 140 guests to lunch.'

In spite of the partners' thriftiness, there was still a gymnastic display, a ceremonial tree-planting and a band. Festivities lasted into the evening.

employees working in them.

This 'grand seigneur' family story is reinforced by a novel set on the estate and first published in the 1920s: A E Mason's *The Prisoner in the Opal,* an irritating, obviously trashy, but quite un-put downable thriller. Mason, who as a wine merchant knew a lot about wine, paid Loudenne a considerable compliment by calling his Château Suvlac 'the most delicate of the second growths'. The château itself is unmistakable, described as 'a rose-pink house of one storey in the shape of a capital E, with two little round towers in the main building and a great stone paved terrace at the back overlooking the River Gironde'. Even the nearest village was called 'St Yzans d'Houlette ' — and the château run, then as now, by a faithful couple, man and wife. But the life he depicts was very different from the peaceful domesticity of Gordon Gilbey or Alec Gold. The house party danced until dawn on their visits during the vendange — a far remove from the dance Gordon Gilbey gave one year for the estate staff to cheer them up. Moreover, the estate was run by a sinister Englishman, who turns out to be an unfrocked priest with a taste for black magic. Unfortunately we have no record of the comments of that doughty Médocain peasant, Camille Gombeau, on his fictional equivalent.

In reality, social life was more muted. The upkeep of the château was naturally neglected during the war, and in 1919 the directors decided that 'in view of the lack of accommodation available at the moment it was decided that ladies should not accompany any party going.' Bayle and Gombeau were authorised to have it repaired and repainted and to spend £2,500 on the buildings on the estate, including the 'erection of a windmill in connection with the water supply', but the château remained fundamentally untouched for half a century after the improvements made to transform it into a residence suitable for Edwardian houseparties. And the only mention of social life are the 'usual' vintage balls; an occasion in 1922 when 'a bottle, perhaps more, was cracked to the bridegroom's health' on the occasion of Alec Gold's forthcoming wedding, and a noticeably restrained celebration of the 50th anniversary of the purchase, when a mere £100 was voted and spent on entertaining 140 guests to lunch (this had to be postponed because Lord Blyth had died in April 1925, almost exactly 50 years after his first visit).

The visits were mostly a record of serious work. In 1919, the most pressing problem was the 'considerable amount of unrest and dissatisfaction among the workpeople', a problem by no means confined to Loudenne, for, as Gordon Gilbey lamented, 'labour is not coming back to the land, as it has always been known to be the worst paid work in France.' Manpower was short — a recurrent problem. During the war, when most of the men had been called up, Lord Blyth had even approached the French Ambassador in London regarding the possible employment of German prisoners-of-war on the estate. Things were not improved by Bayle, 'a great pessimist and does not seem to see a way out of any difficulty whatever. . . a considerable amount of dissatisfaction existing at Loudenne was due to the somewhat abrupt manner in which he deals with the men, and I am led to believe' — doubtless by his old rival Gombeau — 'that several of our old workers left on this account. His great zeal in the Company's interest seems to blind him somewhat in meeting and studying the men as he should, and his way of addressing them I am sure, makes difficulties for himself.'

Gordon Gilbey managed to smooth things over during his first post-war visit in August 1919. His report was apologetic, beginning with the inevitable preamble 'it is always understood at Loudenne that owing to the difficulty of working the heavy soil, we always pay somewhat higher wages than at other properties'. So, after inviting 'a representation of the men one Sunday afternoon at the château', he 'thought it advisable to meet the men to the full extent of their demands'. Gombeau was not forgotten. Before the war he was being paid the then considerable sum of 2000 francs a year, instead of a commission on his sales to French hotels and restaurants, and 'without in any way pressing the point' he persuaded Gordon Gilbey to pay the arrears accumulated during the war, for 'he has never relinquished his interest in this business even during his time in the army and that during the last four or five years a profit of over £1,000 has been made'.

The next May Gordon Gilbey finally established an elaborate system of piece-work, covering virtually every task on the estate. 'After several days of somewhat tedious labour', this was unanimously agreed by the workers — in 1924 the Gilbeys even fell in with the French custom and allowed the workers on the estate a 'sursalaire familial', an allowance to help support their children. For, thanks to Gordon, they were still more deeply involved with their estate than the majority of the Médoc's absentee landlords.

In 1921 the summer was unprecedentedly hot (unfortunately none of the other Gilbeys were as obsessed with the weather as Sir Walter had been, so we don't know the temperature in that famous north-facing room). It was so hot that the wines in one vat reached 100 degrees Fahrenheit — a full 15 degrees more than the maximum permitted today — and the Gilbeys, like every other owner in the Médoc, had extreme problems in controlling the fermentation. Gombeau recommended the oddly-named 'Metaphosphatone', a mixture of 'sulphurous acid and phosphate of ammonia', to try and help the yeasts do their work. Even so they had to sprinkle the grapes with water in order to cool them down as they came in from the fields, and to pump the fermenting juice out of the bottom of the vat, so as to cool it down again before circulating it back in at the top.

They called in a M Mathieu, the director of the Oenological Laboratory of the Gironde, and he advised them to remove the then solid tops of the vats so that the contents could be pumped over the 'châpeau' — the solid mass of grape skins covering the fermentating grape-juice. He also recommended the withdrawal of the wine from the vat as soon as fermentation was complete.

Their problems with the 1921 vintage led Gordon Gilbey and Alec Gold to recommend a truly revolutionary step — the installation of a set of cement vats lined with glass, in which it would be much easier to control fermentation than in the traditional wooden variety. The directors' mood was sufficiently favourable for the work — one of the first in the Médoc — to go ahead after the 1923 vintage. They also invested in equipment to pasteurise some of the wine — for they had found, even before the war, that pasteurised wine was perfectly suitable for the 'A' claret, even though of

MEDULIO
ROYAN
SOULAC
TALAIS
St VIVIEN
QUEYRAC
LESPARRE
GIRONDE
OCÉAN ATLANTIQUE
MEDULIO
St ESTÈPHE
PAUILLAC
St JULIEN
BLAYE
MÉDOC
MOULIS
MARGAUX
MACAU
LUDON
BLANQUEFORT
BORDEAUX
VIN DE LIQUEUR DU MÉDOC
PRODUIT DE FRANCE
VINIFIE ET GARANTI PUR ET D'ORIGINE
PAR LE DOMAINE DE CHÂTEAU LOUDENNE
St YZANS-DE-MÉDOC (GIRONDE)

course such wine did not mature in the bottle.

Nevertheless, even during the relatively prosperous days of the 1920s, the estate was clearly producing more wine than could be sold as such. A number of attempts were made to transform the surplus production into more saleable drinks. After some trouble, it was found possible to use some of the estate's wine, combined with local spirit, to make 'Reo', a fortified drink purveyed by the company in England; and they invested in their own still at Loudenne to make 'marc de Loudenne' from the residue in the vats. In 1928, the directors further demanded that the estate's wine should be transformed into an apéritif 'for which there exists on the Continent a very large demand'.

The result was Gombeau's very own apéritif, Medulio — named after the Latin name for the Médoc, Medius aquae. Gombeau probably got the idea of what might be described as 'port with a sun tan' from the 'Rancio' made in the Pyrenées Orientales. He started by making a raw sort of port — simply done by stopping the fermentation of the grapes through the addition of alcohol. The mixture was then matured by exposing it to the sun. To do so, several thousand clear glass receptacles were designed and ordered. Some of these giant pots, looking rather like giant hospital urine bottles, survive in the museum at Loudenne. In Jasper Grinling's words, 'the wine was then filled into the chambers and loosely corked. On sunny days, up to 2000 receptacles were moved to the front lawn, by hand, for exposure to the sun's rays. When clouds rolled up, or in the evening, they were manhandled back to the chais. Seldom can a more labour-intensive method of production have been devised.'

The result was advertised under the splendid slogan 'Medulio et Vichy sont synonymes de joie et santé'. According to a later régisseur, Charles Bouilleau, it was a 'delicious, supple, rich but not sweet apéritif', and it turned out to be highly successful. Although production stopped in 1937 and was never restarted, the Gilbey management in London was still receiving enquiries for the apéritif in the early 1970s, so the memory obviously lingered on.* At the time Gordon Gilbey's reports were full of optimistic reports on the product. In 1931 he even reported enthusiastically that Schröder and Schÿler, 'a very important Bordeaux house . . . were interesting themselves in the brand', which 'should indicate something useful' — a sad decline from the days, not half a century earlier, when the Gilbeys had been the largest single force in the Bordeaux market.

By then Gordon Gilbey was becoming desperate. In January 1930 the directors minuted a loss of £738 for 1929, and 'in view of the continued decline in the sales of claret, it was decided, as vines went out of bearing, only to renew on those plots where the growth was sufficient to more than repay the cost and generally exercise every possible economy in the conduct of the establishment'. Over succeeding years, the directors' pessimism deepened as the effects of the world slump were compounded by an unprecedented run of three disastrous vintages from 1930

*Medulio has entered mythology. An absconding maître de chai allegedly took the formula away with him, and a mere 20 years ago, a group of workers apparently came across a cask hidden away, among the rubble in the back of a storeroom in the chais. They did not tell their superiors but slipped away until dusk, by which time the cask was empty. The gardener — one of their number — emerged after a terrible night to plant out some lettuce seedlings. Medulio saw to it that they were planted upside down.

to 1932. Nevertheless, Gordon Gilbey remained equal to the challenge. After two visits in October and December 1930 and 'three lengthy meetings' with Gombeau and Bayle, he came up with a package of measures. After noting that 'we have just passed through one of the worst seasons on record for weather', he told the directors that it was impracticable to reduce the estate's production, for 'we should have to uproot the less productive pieces, and we should be left with a property "all patches". Rather than take a drastic step like this at the moment we should endeavour to increase and make better use of the production of the property, which I think can be done.' For until the 1930s they had not apparently been using the estate's own wine for their Château Loudenne brand. 'We have always bought in the Haut-Médoc for this blend. I think we should consider using the Loudenne wine for the Grand Vin mark, and we would not require to buy on the market . . . and sell the surplus of the Loudenne production, if any, on the Bordeaux market with full right to the use of the name "Château Loudenne".'

Gordon fought back by pointing out that 'we have for years taken the production of Loudenne into stock at considerably below its market price, which naturally has more bearing on the accounts than anything else . . . we do not take into stock the value of the spirit we make from the residue of the vintage'. He found a surprising ally in A H Carver (the old accountant's son) who compiled a report after a visit in December 1931. He had found a 'depressing atmosphere that pervaded everywhere, which at first I put down to the damp and dull weather, but I found out later that the chief reason for the depression was that it was thought I had come to Loudenne for the purpose of surveying the property as a prospective purchaser. Rumours had reached Loudenne from London in advance that Gilbey's were selling the property. Generally speaking, the workpeople are depressed and listless, the head men setting the example' — for he, too, had been struck by Bayle's habitual pessimism. The rumour of a prospective sale was reinforced by an alleged offer through the Bordeaux merchants, Bernheim. (It finally emerged that this was a piece of mischief-making directed against Gombeau by a traveller whom he had sacked as an economy measure.)

Carver was not optimistic. He found all the buildings dirty and dilapidated, 'which has also a depressing effect on the staff'. The heart of the matter was psychological; 'If once the staff realised that their employers were again taking an interest in the property they should throw off their lethargy and work with a will to make the sale of Medulio a success'. His solution was increased production through the use of a tractor to cultivate the vineyard; and, after a lightning emergency visit later that month, Gordon Gilbey proposed that they uproot every other row of vines and use a tractor to cultivate the remaining vines more intensively.

The results were immediate. In late February 1931 he was able to report that 'the caterpillar tractor exceeded all my expectations. I look to a wonderful change in the working of the vineyard', which had been reduced by half to a mere 44 acres — less even than it had been when the property was first bought. The staff had been severely cut back, with only eight men in the chais, now shipping a few hundred hogsheads annually, By the following year they had cut out the vegetable garden and 'lost the services of the woman and man who used to keep house on our visits', so he 'arranged to engage a gardener, who can wait at table, and his wife, who can cook'. There were to be fewer animals, too — two pairs of oxen instead of five, and three horses instead of seven.

The directors were, however, relentless. During Gordon Gilbey's visit in May 1932, fire broke out in one of the turret rooms. He recorded 'that had it not been for the wonderful work of the staff the fire would not have been confined to the pavilion. They worked splendidly and intelligently.' The directors were not so grateful. According to family legend, they were furious — Gordon Gilbey should have let the château burn down so that they could claim for the whole insured value, far greater than its worth in the depressed 1930s.

By 1933 he could report further progress, especially in the estate's production. That year, the first to produce acceptable wine since 1929, the yield was 19 hogsheads per hectare (roughly the maximum yield permitted today for an estate of Loudenne's quality). But the general quality was not great, since much of the vineyard was planted either in rather inferior white grapes or, even worse, the baco variety, which had been chosen to ripen early enough to provide a low-grade wine for the vintagers to drink.

Despite Gordon's efforts and the reduction in costs and losses resulting from his efforts, one last threat remained. In May 1936 Anthony Grinling proposed, and Alec Gold seconded, the proposition that 'failing a purchaser of the property being meantime obtained, after the 1937 vintage has been gathered and dealt with, the estate be no longer cultivated as vineyards'. This was agreed, but Henry Walter went one stage further: he would have preferred the death sentence to be pronounced after the 1936 vintage had been dealt with. But even that threat was averted. Fifteen months later, in the nick of time, the directors agreed that 'in consequence of the greatly reduced quantity produced at Loudenne compared with last year, with the resultant shortage of stocks the committee recommended that the decision arrived at in May 1936 be not acted upon but that the vineyard be cultivated for a further year'. So Gordon Gilbey fought, year by year, reducing the loss for 1938 to a mere £980 against £1,500 for 1937, a poor year, largely because of 'the adverse exchange rate and the scanty vintage obtained'.

Even he became powerless to help further when the Germans occupied the Médoc in June 1940. Inevitably the estate interested them, since it was enemy property and thus a legitimate target for an occupier generally determined to behave — in this corner of France anyway — as punctiliously as possible. The Germans bought wines from the estate, crediting the price to an account they opened in the name of W & A Gilbey at a local bank. They did the same with the firm's considerable stocks of cognac, and the directors were understandably delighted when they found these nest eggs credited to their account when the war was over.

Inevitably there are variations in the story of Loudenne in wartime, most noticeably concerning the private cellar containing the most precious bottles on the property. According to the official version, as told to Jasper Grinling, this was walled up, plastered over, and 'distressed' to look old. The Germans, so the story goes, never discovered the cache, and, in 1945 it was ceremoniously unblocked, its contents unharmed by their four-year entombment. John Patrick, another long-serving Gilbey director, heard another version from Gombeau himself. In this one, the old régisseur found the Germans about to help themselves, and flew into a rage, telling them 'if my directors in London knew about this they would be furious', and threatening to tell the soldiers' superiors, thus ensuring that they would be sent to Russia, and away from one of the most agreeable postings in the German armed forces.

The Germans requisitioned the château as an administrative centre from which to direct their attempts to increase food production in the Médoc. After the war, Madame Gombeau, who was in charge of the château itself, told Jasper Grinling how 'an inspection party appeared on the doorstep. Madame Gombeau had a few moments' warning of their arrival. She rushed to the farm, gathered rat droppings, and distributed them liberally throughout the château, particularly in the bedrooms' — another has it that she was trying to deter them from using the château as an offical army brothel. 'But the inspecting officers were not sufficiently deterred by this gallant act of domestic resistance', and for the next four years the château was fully occupied by a certain Captain Blank and a number of orderlies.

As Jasper Grinling heard the story after the war:

'Herr Kapitain Blank and his staff began to address themselves to increasing food and fuel supplies, within their administrative zone, in the face of French non-cooperation. Loudenne, where they lived, became an example. Camille Gombeau and, initially, George Bayle, were told to uproot vineyards to plant cereal crops in their place; mature trees were to be felled for fuel. To these instructions Gombeau and Bayle complied with as much subtle inactivity and counter-argument as possible, just short of provoking their own deportation.

'Some vines, in the least favoured areas, were slowly grubbed out to be replaced by thin cereals grown on unsuited soils; and part of the wood at the heart of the estate was felled to the ground.

'One remote Court of Appeal was available to them — the Bureau de Sequestration in Paris. The 'Sequestre' for the Bordeaux area, 'Bobby' Schneider, once visited Loudenne in person to adjudicate between occupiers and occupied. Gombeau complained, needless to say, about everything. Herr Schneider was married to a Frenchwoman and thus was in a difficult position, as the two wives agreed. So little was changed to improve conditions.

'After the war, Herr Schneider returned to Germany, where, in due course, he became the import agent for Croft Port*. The infinite displeaure, often expressed, of Camille Gombeau when this news travelled back to Loudenne, became part of the family folklore.'

The atmosphere at Loudenne during the occupation was explained by Madame Gombeau to Jack Lambert, then

*Even earlier, in 1947, he had turned up at Loudenne and foisted himself for tea on an embarrassed John Gilbey and his wife.

writing for *The Sunday Times,* when he visited Loudenne in 1958: 'Just as we were going to have lunch there was a knock at the door. I went. It was a German officer. ''I want some lunch'', he said. My husband came. ''There is a hotel in St Yzans, three kilometres away'', he said. ''Yes'', said the German, ''but I want some lunch here.'' What could we do? They were all well behaved, except that they would put their feet up on these chaises-longues, and every Saturday afternoon would give a tea party. Their friends would motor out, from Bordeaux even, and when the weather was fine they would sit in groups on the terrace.'

'What did they do?'

'But nothing, absolutely nothing. It was pleasant for them.'

These stories do not entirely do justice to Gombeau's stubborn defence of the Gilbeys' interests. In the words of Gordon Gilbey's son John (now Lord Vaux), 'it was a miracle that Gombeau was not shot. Anything that he didn't like he said to the German officer in charge, ''Mr Gordon wouldn't do that; so I can't do it.'' Nine times out of ten he got away with it.'

Even without the German harassment, the vintages of the years of occupation were dreadfully difficult because of a shortage of fuel for the tractors and labour for picking.

Camille Gombeau told Jasper Grinling how he had disinterred a crumbling pony trap, imported to Loudenne by the Gilbeys in Victorian times, and made this his means of getting around. Such wines as were produced were allowed to be sold through local trade channels. Indeed, without the money from these sales, the income of the estate would have been reduced to zero and nothing would have been available to pay the few workers left on the estate.

But these sales meant that, when Gordon Gilbey finally managed to visit Loudenne only a few months after the end of the war, he found that there was no stock with which to finance the repairs the estate needed so urgently; and strict foreign exchange regulations prevented the directors from investing more than the most nominal sums for the next 15 years.

In the meantime the battle of Loudenne continued, despite the death of the octogenarian Henry Walter Gilbey in 1945. In March 1945, Gombeau was told to replant only the best ground, and, early the following year, the directors are recorded as being prepared to consider 'any definite offer received through M Dury of the Banque de Commerce et de l'Industrie'. This came to nothing. In November that year Gombeau's salary was raised to £400 a year, and he was granted a gift of 100,000 francs (plus £50 for his wife) for their stalwart efforts during the war.

But most of the post-war minutes could have been written at any time during the previous half-century. In November 1946 Gombeau was to spell out the cost of improving the estate to set against a possible sale price, and was to return to the old practice of buying wines direct from the growers rather than from the trade. Replanting slowly gathered momentum, and a deputy was appointed 'subject to his wife being considered suitable to act as hostess, when necessary'. Almost immediately, two emissaries had to be despatched to London, because Gombeau had quarrelled with the 'foreman of the estate'. By 1949 Gordon Gilbey claimed, for the umpteenth time, that he had analysed the position and the figures were better than was thought at first. As a result, Gombeau was authorised to spend up to £3,500 for doing up the château and the farm, a further £500 on a white wine press, and £75 for a 'sulphuring machine for the vines'.

By then Gombeau was in his 70s and Gordon Gilbey — with the help of his son John — had to grapple with the problem of succession. Gombeau had become a (not totally loved) local legend: his rather nasal intonation was widely imitated and his liaison with his maid a matter of routine village gossip. But none of the three potential successors hired after the war could get on with him — or, more significantly, with Madame Gombeau, widely thought to have a deciding voice in the household.

During the war Bayle's place had been taken by his daughter. In 1945 she was succeeded by a man called Bourricot. But he did not last, for in 1947 Gordon Gilbey 'had the pleasure of welcoming Mr and Mrs Pierre Neel to Loudenne, from whom we hope great things'. His position became less clear when a young man called Menotti was appointed a 'sous-régisseur' in 1949 and described, two years later, as 'a recent and very competent addition to the staff'. But they both quarrelled with Gombeau. John Gilbey remembers how he and Bassy's son Arthur had to fly to Bordeaux in a specially chartered light aircraft to sort out a row between Gombeau and one of them. In theory, Gombeau was going to retire to take on his uncle's property in Normandy. So, in 1953, a local man, Charles Bouilleau, was appointed to run the vineyard in the place of Neel, who had got across both Menotti and Gombeau. Bouilleau was the first post-war appointee to have run an estate. (He came to Gombeau's notice when he was restoring Château La Cardonne and two other properties near Loudenne, a vital qualification since Gombeau himself knew next to nothing about viticulture*). Bouilleau soon started to reorganise the vineyard, repairing the numerous implements left in the fields to rust over the years, and installing a proper system of piece-work and work study. In 1954 Bassy visited Loudenne; did not like what he saw; and, on his return to London, the directors dismissed Menotti, leaving Bouilleau as Gombeau's heir apparent. In the event he stayed on at Loudenne until 1972, going on to run a number of other major châteaux in the area.

Bouilleau's arrival was only one element in the reawakening of Loudenne after the war. According to his son, Gordon Gilbey's proudest moment in all his long association with Loudenne came soon after the war, when the feast of St Vincent — a major event in the Médoc — was celebrated in the little church at St Yzans. Gordon's elder son Peter, a Benedictine monk, said mass, served by John Gilbey, before a congregation which included the local Cardinal as well as local lay dignitaries like the Prefect of the Gironde.

The Gilbeys' first attempt to open the château to outsiders after the war came with a press visit in 1952. John Patrick remembers it as a 'vague attempt to show people Loudenne. It was rather embarrasssing as the property was in such a terrible state.' In the event, the press trip — and subsequent visits by individual journalists — did indeed generate favourable publicity, for the house had not entirely

*Perhaps more importantly, Bouilleau was a man born and bred in the region — a Médocain from the next village to Gombeau's own.

lost its appeal, well captured by Phillip Youngman Carter, an early post-war writer, in his book, *On to Andorra.* 'The house had an odd, highly individual charm. The elegant rooms, with their long garden windows, are faded and shabby with the air of an empty children's nursery, where the toys have only lately been tidied. Random possessions seem to have taken up residence in established positions. I half expected my old nurse Ruth to look in to make sure I was going to sleep.' Jack Lambert noted the little upright piano in the 'pearl-grey, faded salon . . . in a cupboard sit, hopefully, piles of English prayer-books . . . and in the small drawing room next door are bookshelves which should be kept as they are, so perfectly do their contents mirror the light fading of other ages . . . *Racing Up-To-Date* (1906); P C Wren; E Phillips Oppenheim; *Hunting, Shooting and Fishing: a Sporting Miscellany,* 1877 — all still perfectly preserved.'

The press visit of 1952. Below: Gordon Gilbey's 'proudest moment' — the celebration of mass by his son Peter in the presence of the local Cardinal.

To less remote souls, the sheer inconvenience of the house was its most obvious fault. It was habitable only in the summer; at other times the Gilbeys had to stay in Bordeaux, and commute every day. The neglect of half a century was indeed beginning to catch up. As Jasper Grinling remembers: 'The property continued to crumble quietly away. White ants invaded the timber structures of the chais, still lit only by paraffin lamps; a fire broke out in part of the roof of the château; in winter, water ran down the inside of the walls; the only method of obtaining bath water was from a copper cylinder heated by sticks of wood; chickens ran around the kitchen; the baize of the Russian billiard table mouldered to dust; not a note of the piano could produce a sound; the plaster fell off the outside walls; and only four of the dining room chairs were any longer safe to sit on.' (John Patrick indeed remembers two antique chairs collapsing under the weight of Bassy and Camille Gombeau).

During the 1950s very little was accomplished. However, John Patrick, who, in his own words, 'originally went out there largely to act as baggage boy and to play golf at Bordeaux with Bassy', remembers Gombeau (who never did retire) 'sitting in his tiny office above the garage puffing away at that pipe of his stuffed with black tobacco, arguing day after day with Gordon Gilbey, arguing interminably about the termites in the chais, with Gordon claiming that there was simply not enough money to do them up'.

In February 1957, Gordon Gilbey wrote a moving note in the visitors' book. 'With great grief I record the passing away of Camille Gombeau. For more than fifty years he has managed Château Loudenne and both he and his charming wife have acted as wonderful hosts to all directors on their visits. He will be greatly missed by all the directors and friends and by nobody more than myself who has worked with him for fifty years less two. I mourn the death of a good colleague and friend.' Within three months he had an even more poignant note to append: 'Looking back 47 years in this book of visits I am reminded of my wife's first visit to Loudenne on our honeymoon. I must painfully record today her passing away on May 11th.'

An era had ended.

RENAISSANCE

The decade after Gombeau's death was revolutionary for the château itself, for the estate, and for the commercial role of Loudenne. Charles Bouilleau's brother, Alain, arrived as régisseur in 1959 to supervise the estate from the little corner office designed for that purpose a century before. He found 24 hectares (60 acres) under vines — about the same amount as the Gilbeys had found when they bought the estate in 1875. And, worse, the outlook after the war had been so poor that white grape varieties had been planted on land reserved for, and entitled to, Loudenne appellation. Even in areas reserved for red wine there was a strange mixture of varieties. The famous 1961 vintage, for instance, was made from a mere 12 hectares of vines, of which nearly 80 per cent was merlot, and the bulk of the rest malbec and petit verdot — an extraordinary mixture. Yet he quickly learnt that, as he put it, 'on Loudenne's rather rich soil it is important not to have too much cabernet sauvignon because the wine wouldn't be drinkable for twenty five years'. He worked at replanting and extending the vineyard under the direction of John Patrick, the firm's first non-family management trainee, who was largely responsible for Loudenne in the late 1950s and early 1960s.

Bouilleau, encouraged by Patrick, instituted a complete replanting programme: as a result of their planting in the '60s, the estate now has well over 100 acres under vines, two-thirds of it destined to make red wine. Even today, however, the cabernet sauvignon by no means dominates the vineyard. Although half the vineyard is planted with red wine varieties, the more productive merlot provides up to 50 per cent of the grapes required for the 'grand vin' — an unusually high percentage for a vineyard in the Médoc. The white wine varieties, semillon and sauvignon, have been relegated to 15 hectares of peripheral land*, very little of it entitled to the valuable 'Haut-Médoc' appellation.

In London, Patrick was working with his colleague David Peppercorn to resurrect Loudenne's contacts with the Bordeaux trade, links dormant for generations because of the decline in claret-drinking in Britain. Peppercorn, arguably the possessor of the finest palate in the Gilbeys' service since the heyday of Jim Blyth, was not a member of one of the founding families. But his father had become the Gilbeys' first non-family director in the late 1950s, following the takeover of his family firm, so that his son's views at least reached the Gilbey board room.

The two youngsters, emulating their predecessors, found a trusty broker to work with them. Like George Merman before him, Jean-Paul Gardère is based not in Bordeaux, but — in this case — in Pauillac. Gardère, loquacious, a notable raconteur, relishes his role as the 'archetypal Médocain', but underneath the music-hall exterior of a country character lies one of the shrewdest brains in the business — a talent recognised by the Pearson family when they bought control of Château Latour in 1962 and appointed Gardère a director a year later. He proved invaluable for Patrick and Peppercorn in re-establishing links with the Bordeaux trade, which were duly appreciative of the new attentions. 'Some of the older generation hadn't been to Loudenne for forty years', says Patrick, but they all felt 'even the Chartronnais don't receive you like this'.

*This includes the excellent gravelly slopes forming the river bank itself, which is too close to the water for the French authorities to allow it the full 'appellation', despite the quality of the soil.

This page: £100,000 had to be spent simply to prevent the estate from crumbling into ruin. Overleaf: The château and chais reroofed, rewired and renewed.

Patrick emphasises that the revitalised role of Loudenne 'stemmed from the redecoration'. This was not a minor matter: nearly £100,000 had to be spent simply to prevent the château from crumbling into ruin. True to form, the decision was made almost by accident after yet another attempt by the 'antis' to sell the château, at a time when 'pieds noirs', Frenchmen from Algeria, were buying all over the Médoc. The board minutes for 23 September 1960 note how Robin Gold 'mentioned that he heard that, particularly in view of the present political situation in Algeria, there might be a possibility of disposing of the property at Loudenne on advantageous terms. It was agreed that the Hon J H P Gilbey should arrange for the property to be valued and that it might be put about that we would not entirely be disinterested in any offers that might be made. Simultaneously a more exact estimate of its worth to the business will be made.'

But John Gilbey had learnt from his father how to cope with threats like that, largely by establishing that the estate's market value turned out to be low. He also found a natural ally in Jasper Grinling, then design and production director, and at that time responsible for the move of the firm's warehouses and cellars from Camden Town to Harlow New Town. Between them, they persuaded the board to provide the finance for the now-inescapable restoration of Loudenne. This included reroofing, rewiring, installing proper central heating, renewing the plumbing, and installing an extra bathroom. Even more fundamental was the need to deal with the damp. Its past effects were excised and the exterior then rendered in its present pale-pink stucco. Then came the problem of the interior and its furnishings. In Grinling's words: 'By this time the sum of money authorised had grown perilously small. The château had never been more than sparsely furnished at best, for the most part with heavy and ornate Edwardian pieces, which early Gilbeys had, idosyncratically, ordered from Switzerland. With the help of a decorator, Mme Chollet, from Paris, who appeared ready to take on the interior with a minimal budget; with some furniture, lamps, pictures, materials and objects shipped from London; and finally with the contents of a linen cupboard bought in Bordeaux, the renovated château came slowly to life. A date was set for a first "Loudenne party" in the autumn of 1963, only a few months following the formation of IDV. Celebratory bottles were opened; pictures were hung; and, as could be relied upon, the pervasive charm of Loudenne began to work its magic upon the enlarged circle of its proprietors. The pro-faction appeared to be safely in the ascendancy. The immediate crisis was over.'

The refurbishing of the vineyard and the château itself was only the initial step in remedying the effects of over half a century of neglect. 'The next step', in Jasper Grinling's words, 'was to remedy the neglected accommodation for the resident work-force. This had scarcely changed since the Victorian age. Sanitation, running water and heating in the cottages was either non-existent or substandard. Again, typically, the enlarged board of IDV plunged itself into introspective debate in the early months of 1967 as to whether to build new cottages or to sell out. A Bordeaux valuer was asked to declare what the entire estate would fetch on the open market, if the 15 cottages were built for £85,000. He came up with the surprisingly modest figures of £300,000 — only some 10 times greater than the purchase price of the château 92 years earlier. Armed with this additional ammunition, the pros and the antis again ranged sides. In the event Loudenne survived. The new cottages went ahead, to the design of Thurloe Connolly, a young Irish architect. The Secretary to the Board in London, on 19th January, 1967 — no doubt having listened to argument and counter-argument on the Loudenne battlefield more than a few times before — contented himself with recording the final skirmish over decent accommodation for those working at Loudenne in these words: "The final decision on the future of the Château will be made by a judgement of the management, and not necessarily supported by prospects of profit." '

By that time, the pro-Loudenne faction was enjoying, albeit temporarily, an ascendancy not seen since the 1880s. Even Walter Gilbey, the finance director and son of 'The Champion', the archetypal persecutor of the Loudennites, had cheerfully organised funds for the new cottages. True to his grandfather's obsession, he became deeply involved in ensuring that the farmland on the other side of the road was not neglected, did not revert to marshland suitable only for letting as rough shooting, and was properly drained and used for growing hay and cereals.

The 'enlarged board' referred to by Jasper Grinling contained a new Loudenne enthusiast, Geoffrey Hallowes, whose family firm, Twiss & Brownings & Hallowes, was one of three constituents of the IDV group. Francophile and married to the resistance heroine, Odette Churchill, Hallowes had an affection for Loudenne, and it was his

choice to send a new recruit, Martin Bamford, to run the group's interests in France, including Loudenne, in 1968, largely because he was a bachelor. Martin's first action was typical of what was to come. A couple of years before his arrival, the old wooden doors of the chais had been replaced with some incongruous steel roller blinds, which jarred with the 19th-century stonework. Martin promptly had them taken down and replaced with doors modelled on the original pattern; at the same time, and seemingly without permission, he spent a substantial sum of money replacing the clock above the chais and on the meticulous restoration of the tower which housed it. Clearly, mere budgetary considerations did not loom over-large to Loudenne's new overseer.

But commercial — if not financial — considerations certainly played a larger part in Martin Bamford's life than many of his friends suspected. Initially, he worked with David Peppercorn in devising a plan for exploiting Loudenne more fully as a commercial centre, but the framework within which he was operating soon became infinitely more rigid and restrictive. After a determined and successful attempt in the mid-1960s to ward off one unwelcome bidder, in the shape of the Showering family, IDV succumbed at the beginning of the 1970s to an even more unwelcome bid from Watneys, who themselves were promptly taken over by Grand Metropolitan Hotels.

Martin survived these disturbances like the viceroy of a distant colony insulated from successive revolutions in the imperial capital. Nevertheless, the change of ownership represented a major break with the history of Loudenne since 1875. Throughout the 1970s Martin became accountable to the professional standards of one of Britain's largest and best-run companies. He was lucky in finding tacit support from Sir Maxwell Joseph, chairman of Grand Metropolitan until his death in 1982 (eerily, only two days before Martin's). 'MJ' responded to the magic of Loudenne — and certainly enjoyed drinking its wines.

Nevertheless, Martin had to justify Loudenne's position, by producing, not only wines, but also ideas for new products. He succeeded. In the words of Francis Fouquet, who has run the commercial side of Loudenne since 1974, 'Martin was the architect of an entirely new commercial policy, designed to emphasise a brand name rather than the name of the producer. For instance, our branded claret was called "La Cour Pavillon", with little or no mention of the Gilbey name.' Martin had equally strong ideas about what his new brand should taste like, and put them into practice with the help of Jean-Louis Camps, a brillant young oenologist he brought over from Burgundy — itself a revolutionary step in French wine circles. Their latest product, 'Les Chais', a table wine with all the qualities of a minor claret, was being launched when Martin died.

Martin also involved his employers in the early 1970s in the system of 'exclusivities', by which château owners entrusted the sale of all their wine to one firm of merchants. When the boom in claret collapsed, leaving everyone in Bordeaux with enormous and unsaleable stocks of often very fine wines, Martin was equal to the occasion. Where other firms resorted to the salerooms, Martin reverted to the techniques which had made the Gilbey fortune in the first place — an ingenious offer which no-one could refuse. Advertisements were placed in *The Times* and the *Financial*

Times in early 1975. Dressed up as a 'Unique Centenary Sale' of fine wines lodged at Loudenne, the scheme provided drinkers with a gamble. A quiz was included; all respondents paying a set sum received 10 cases of decent claret; the better the answer, the better the wine.

Out of the carnage of 1974 – 5, Martin retained only two 'exclusivities' — the classed growth Château Giscours, and the fine bourgeois wine Château de Pez — but managed to remain friends even with the owners of the château whose wines he was no longer buying. With Robert Duson of Pez he devised a fascinating experiment: to set aside a small barrique of each of the three varieties — merlot, cabernet franc and cabernet sauvignon — which made up the finished wine, and to keep it over the years. Tasting the separate 'cépages' provided an unequalled opportunity to understand the importance of the 'assemblages' of the different cépages, and to appreciate the very specific contribution made by each one.

Obviously Martin was involved in the estate's own wine. His particular pride was the white: once the very latest in stainless steel low-temperature fermentation vats had been installed, Loudenne Blanc could be counted with the handful of other great dry white wines of Bordeaux.

Sadly, many of Martin's guests did not fully appreciate his expert, detailed and passionate concern for the estate as a commercial and viticultural entity — he was a great one for compartmentalising his life. Virtually no building on the estate escaped Martin's attention — even the former hen-house between the house and the chais, which had become an office, was transformed into an ideal tasting-room, a simple chapel in which to worship the holy grape. Throughout the 1970s he worked with Thurloe Connolly, not so much to restore the interior of Loudenne's buildings as to create an atmosphere blending old and new, as the estate as a whole blends French and English elements.

The reconstruction work extended from the garages to the little towers. These were transformed into charming apartments, one for Martin and the other for a series of 'chatelaines'. These redoubtable ladies coped, usually successfully, with the ferocious schedule imposed by Martin, ensuring that every detail, from the appropriate flags to welcome every nationality under the sun, to magazines on the salon table, was correct*.

The bedrooms in the main part of the house were restored and provided with individual bathrooms — one, at least, all in brown wood with a free-standing bath, worthy of the country house of some 18th-century aristocrat. The former chapel, used by the Gilbeys as a sort of men's dormitory, had fallen into disuse, and became a delighful library, housing the château's most precious volumes. The hundreds of other wine books acquired over the years were lodged in the famous north-facing reading room where the first Sir Walter Gilbey had spent so many happy hours pondering the mysteries of Loudenne's weather. The main salon was redecorated in pale Adam-green, with completely new furniture — the solid old chaises-longues were banished to a visitors' reception in the chais, deliberately designed to resemble a Victorian drawing-room.

The chais themselves were restored to their pristine

*My first impression of Loudenne was that it was the only château in the Médoc where *Country Life* and *Private Eye* jostled for attention.

Overleaf: Martin Bamford sensitively inserted a new staircase in the chais, 'blending old and new'; he also 'assembled a unique collection of old viticultural implements'. Above: The old henhouse was 'transformed into an ideal tasting room'.

splendour; and with the help of Alain Bouilleau, Martin assembled a unique collection of old viticultural implements. The collection has now outgrown its accommodation, and plans for its expansion were going through at the time of Martin's death. The wing nearest the chais was gutted and its exterior restored in the correct 18th-century idiom, while the interior was remodelled in an airy modern style.

But the finest achievement of the Connolly-Bamford duo was the restoration of the former vintage kitchen. Martin unearthed the splendidly massive old copper ranges, whose contents had so intrigued Beatty Kingston. They were restored, handsome and practical cherrywood cupboards and shelves installed, the kitchen was painted, and the whole opened in July 1980 with a flourish and a feast by Robert Carrier. Since then the kitchen has been used everyday as a canteen for the staff at Loudenne, together with any casual visitors feeling the need for an absurdly cheap and delicious lunch, as well as for more formal occasions.

His greatest contribution was to the feeling of the château. 'He inherited an impersonal house', says Jean-Paul Gardère simply, 'and gave it life'.

Martin was at his best — witty, thoughtful, self-deprecatory — on informal occasions, enjoying the 'glass of fizz' which punctuated so many such sessions, sitting on the terrace of a long summer evening with his friends, discussing Cat's latest absurdity, or some new addition to the delights of Loudenne, or eating a meal (perhaps one he himself had cooked) in the little summer house tucked away at one end of the terrace. In his last newsletter from Loudenne, he mentions a typical visit by the American cookery writer, Julia Child. 'In the vintage kitchen', he wrote, 'fresh marinated sardines and an aloyau of beef grilled on vine branches took the strain, together with a spectacular bottle of Loudenne 1971. It was a perfect day.'

Martin provided many such 'perfect days' for his friends. He restored to Loudenne the same welcoming atmosphere, the same mixture of simplicity and cosiness which had pervaded the château in the first years of the Gilbeys' ownership. He even provided the modern equivalent of the 'smart English omnibus' which had greeted Somerville and Ross on their arrival at Lesparre station. Nowadays a chauffeur driven car meets visitors to Loudenne at

Bordeaux airport. The chauffeur, Albert, is instantly recognisable by his grey uniform and peaked cap. Martin would never allow Albert to greet visitors in 'civvies'. To Martin everything connected with Loudenne had to be stylish and correct, and everyone connected with the estate had to perform his or her role impeccably. Martin's attitude was very similar to that of the first Sir Walter Gilbey, who in his day had been equally determined to stamp his personality on Loudenne.

Yet where Sir Walter, particularly in his later years, was surrounded only by a crowd of cronies and hangers-on, Martin was a personal friend of most of the leading figures in the international world of wine, and it was always assumed that writers, merchants, brokers, anyone from anywhere in the world interested in the fine wines of Bordeaux, would somehow find their way at regular intervals to Loudenne. There they shared not only the superb wine and food provided by Josette, arguably the region's finest cook, but also Martin's passion for perfection. This did not necessarily imply the most expensive. As Pamela Vandyke Price noted in an obituary, 'everything gave his friends standards of quality to delight in, whether it was the flower on the breakfast tray or an arrangement of just "some cold meat and salad" as beautiful as any Chardin still-life'.

It was as a professional in an exacting world that Martin was admired in the Médoc itself. He died during the vintage, the most tense and preoccupying time of year, yet over 200 château-owners, régisseurs and maîtres de chai, merchants, brokers and friends attended his funeral at the little village church at St Yzans. It was entirely appropriate

Far left: The vintage kitchen before and after restoration. Left: 'Martin unearthed the splendidly massive old copper ranges'. Above: 'The salon was redecorated in pale Adam-green, with completely new furniture'. Below: Martin Bamford and 'Cat'.

that he should have been buried between the graves of two vignerons in a village cemetery surrounded by vines.

But Martin's true memorial is Château Loudenne's indestructible warmth and friendliness. Many a visitor could echo the words written in an earlier visitors' book by Mr H Kains Jackson, of 109 Cheyne Walk, Chelsea, who, on 22 September 1884, 'came unfriended, solitary, alone, to find an old château and old friends'.

ACKNOWLEDGEMENTS

This book would never have seen the light of day without the initial impetus provided by Martin Bamford and the steadfast support of Jasper Grinling at Grand Metropolitan and Tom Jago at IDV. I am grateful, too, to John Patrick and to Lord Vaux for reading the first draft and bearing patiently with my sometimes acerbic remarks about his family. Monsignor Alfred Gilbey was a mine of information, and steered me towards the quotation from Anthony Trollope on page 28. My researches among the Gilbey archives were greatly helped by John Dadd at York Gate and Chris Snowden at Harlow. At Loudenne, the present chatelaine, Luce Navel, together with Sylvain, Josette and Albert, made me more than welcome, and Francois Fouquet, Jean-Louis Camps, Charles and Alain Bouilleau were most helpful. Walter Gilbey kindly gave me access to the family documents and photographs stored at Rose Hill, Henley.

Mr Dave Gutzke of the University of Toronto provided me with useful information regarding the Gilbeys' political activities from his forthcoming thesis on the subject. Pamela Prior kindly unearthed a great deal of information about Edouard Brown from the French archives. Rebecca Faith provided me with an invaluable analysis of Loudenne's visitors and the Gilbeys' sales figures over a period of fifty years. Mrs Deborah Allan somehow deciphered my manuscript and transformed it into a proper book. It was subsequently impeccably edited and produced by Tim Rock and Kathy Lambert.

The sources of this book are primarily the Loudenne Diary, which was transcribed some time ago, the Travelling Journal for 1874, and the account and letter books, all preserved at Loudenne. They were supplemented by the Directors' minute books at 1 York Gate — which include the minutes of the Loudenne sub-Committee — and a wide variety of other documents housed at Harlow, including the important confidential letters sent out so regularly in the last forty years of the 19th century.

For the secondary sources are inadequate. The most recent work in the field, Brian Harrison's *Drink and the Victorians,* is useful mainly to those interested in the temperance movement. The family history — *Half a Century of Successful Trade* by Sir Herbert Maxwell, published privately in 1907 — is a good example of its kind, but obviously does not provide a full account. *Merchants of Wine* by Alec Waugh, published in 1957, adds little or nothing to Maxwell's account. Thus it was natural for the late Alec Gold to wish to supplement the account it provided; his *Four-in-Hand,* published the same year, provides an invaluable genealogy of all four families.

My thanks are due to the following for permission to reproduce their illustrations: Photographie Burdin, 108; Jasper Grinling, 59, 66 – 67 (a view of Loudenne from the Gironde painted by his grandmother, Mrs Gibbons Grinling); Michel Guillard, title page, 9, 12, 13, 153; Michael Kuh, 158, 159; J S Gray, 23; Christopher Wood Gallery, 31 ('The Public Bar' by John Henry Henshall). The engravings on pages 33, 35, 36, 37, 39 and 55 are from *The Illustrated London News*; that on page 32 is by Thomas Shepherd; and the photographs on pages 71, 74, 82 and 130 were taken by Sir Benjamin Stone in 1908. The balance has been drawn largely from IDV's extensive archives, with the tireless help of Jasper Grinling and the late Martin Bamford.